COLLECTING SPORTING ART

Collecting
SPORTING ART
Edited by JNP WATSON

Foreword by

The Duke of Beaufort

° THE °
SPORTSMAN'S
PRESS
LONDON

Published by
The Sportsman's Press 1988

© The Sportsman's Press Ltd 1988

British Library Cataloguing in Publication Data

Collecting sporting art.
    1. British visual arts. Special subjects.
Sports
I. Watson, J. N. P. (John N. P.)
704.9′49796

ISBN 0-948253-22-3

Photoset and printed in Great Britain by
BAS Printers Limited, Over Wallop, Hampshire

CONTENTS

ACKNOWLEDGEMENTS

The editor, contributors and publishers are grateful to the following for permission to reproduce the pictures. References are to page numbers; **bold** figures indicate plate numbers.

Arthur Ackermann & Sons Ltd 10, 15, 23, 26, 29, 30, 31, 46, 50, 51, 53, 54, 55, 56, 57, 60, 62, 63, 65, 66, 67, 69, 71, 72, 108, 110, 111, 112, 113, 116, 118, 132, 135, 136, 138, 139, 152; **2** (above), **10** (below).
British Sporting Art Trust 126, 149, 150
Brotherton Gallery **14** (above)
Christie's Fine Arts **5** (above), **11, 17, 19** (above)
Robert Fountain **19** (below)
Richard Green Gallery 122, 124, 125, 127, 128, 129; **3, 4, 6, 8,** (above), **9** (above), **21** (below)
HM The Queen 13, 33
HM Queen Elizabeth the Queen Mother 150
Hobhouse Ltd, 134
Sladmore Gallery 97, 98, 99, 100, 101, 102, 103, 104, 105; **16**
Sotheby's 115; **1, 7** (above)
Spinks **14** (below)
Sporting and Wildlife Painting 90
Tate Gallery 146, 148; **8** (below)
Tryon Gallery 40, 43, 44, 74, 76, 85, 86, 87, 88, 89, 91, 92, 119, 142 (top); **15**
Walters Art Gallery, Baltimore 94
Yale Centre for British Art, Paul Mellon Collection 19, 106, 120, 127

The publishers would also like to thank Sally Mitchell for allowing them to use her book *The Dictionary of Equestrian Artists* in their research.

FOREWORD BY
HIS GRACE THE DUKE OF BEAUFORT

When I joined Marlborough Fine Art in 1949, art dealing was considered by some of the more narrow-minded of the older generation to be not quite the thing. I well remember being asked: 'What do you sell? Sporting prints I suppose?' I rather insinuated that this was the case, which seemed to make it more acceptable to them than selling Picassos. However, things have changed since those days and now everyone's dream is to enter the art business and sell Picasso, or whatever.

In fact, much as I would have liked to, I have not been very much involved in sporting art, except for a few masterpieces which have passed through our hands in the last forty years. I have, however, been lucky enough to have enjoyed my family's considerable collection at Badminton over the years which has given me increasing pleasure. The house is filled with endless pictures of their dogs, horses, ponies, hounds etc., collected through the centuries, all of whom seem much better looking than my ancestors would appear to have been. For instance, Wootton received much patronage from my family who sent him to Rome to study, and the house today contains many of his paintings, which is perhaps the reason why there is no painting by Stubbs in the collection.

Sporting art appeals to all tastes, not just to those actively participating in sporting pursuits – as, indeed, you do not have to be a clergyman to appreciate religious painting of the Renaissance. Likewise, this excellent book will appeal to all who are interested in the arts and who hope to start collecting in however small or large a way.

Beaufort

1

THE COLLECTOR AND
THE STORY OF SPORTING ART

J. N. P. WATSON

J. N. P. Watson, the editor of this book, first took an interest in art
at Eton, under the guidance of Wilfrid Blunt, and later studied at the
City and Guilds of London Art School. During his first career – with the Royal
Horse Guards and the Guards Independent Parachute Company, which he
commanded – he was a polo player, pentathlete, Bisley shot and point-to-point
rider. After being invalided from the Army, John Watson spent 18 years on the
editorial staff of *Country Life* for which he continues as hunting, polo
and animal and sporting art correspondent. Since 1978 he has also been polo
correspondent to *The Times*. The unique number of different hunts
with which he has ridden (or run) has earned him a place in the
Guinness Book of Records. In 1982 he was awarded a Churchill Travelling
Fellowship, in recognition of his writings on animal welfare and
wildlife conservation. He is the author of 14 books.

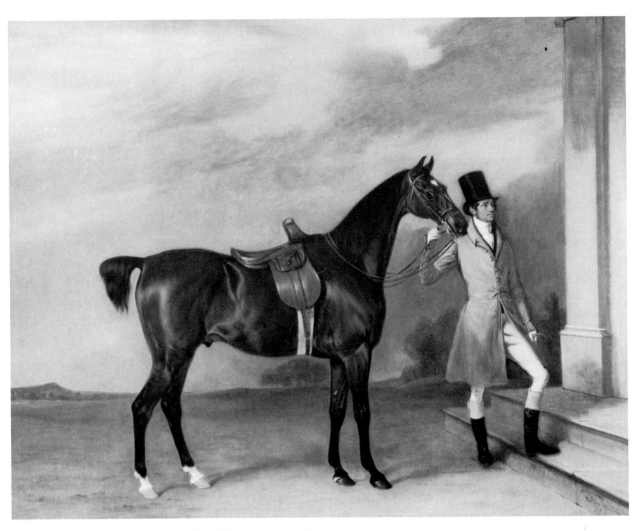

John Ferneley Snr's portrait of Miss Villebois' bay hunter held by a groom, 1834.

Sporting art is primarily, if not uniquely, an English subject and one of the finest things to have come out of the English heritage. The body of interest and admiration for the school of sporting artists is growing and the truly enthusiastic student of the subject can form his or her judgements and tastes when roaming the museums and galleries in Britain, on the Continent (particularly in France and Germany), and in the United States. He can also seek out the sporting pictures at historic houses that are open to the public and attend exhibitions at those gallery salerooms specialising in the subject.

This book is designed not only for the enthusiast who would like to possess a work or two of sporting art, but also for those who are keen to acquire a little more knowledge of the subject for its own sake. The contributors, acknowledged experts in their field, are all deeply and professionally involved in the subjects they are discussing.

Since no country in the world has a stronger tradition of involvement in sport – particularly racing and field sports – than Britain, her wealth of sporting art reflects in great and colourful measure several aspects of British social history. However, the story of sporting art had its roots in man's earliest history, so it is as well to begin with a general survey of the subject from its birth to its present place in the world.

The earliest pictures our world knows, those chalked and painted on cave walls, are mostly of hunters and their quarry. And very animated, fluent, accurate and full of artistic merit most of them are, suggesting that the chase was the chief fertilising agent for the latent creative impulses of our remotest ancestors. To the men of prehistory the rhythm and drama of the hunt was the most aesthetically appealing, as well as the most exciting, subject that they shared with one another and with wild Nature.

When the ancients learned to grow crops and to domesticate and farm cattle and poultry, an element of sport entirely for its own sake came into the pursuit until, by medieval times, hunting was less for food and more a diversion for the rich and powerful, the leisured classes. 'What does a man do when he is free to do as he pleases?' asks the Spanish philosopher, Ortega y Gasset. 'The aristocrat has always done the same things: raced horses or competed in physical exercises, gathered at parties . . . or engaged in conversation. But before any of those, and consistently more important, has been hunting . . . This is what kings and nobles have preferred to do: they have hunted . . .'

Since the eras of the earliest civilizations, Babylonia, Assyria and Egypt, the cults of the horse, hound and hawk in sport, the hunt and the race, were the preserves of high social rank, and hunting was closely connected with war. The Greeks and Romans laid great stress on sport of every kind, but especially hunting, as a preparation for fighting. The Greek general, Xenophon, wrote the world's first treatise on the chase, *Cynegeticus. Noblesse oblige*, princes and noblemen commanded from the front in battle, and they were expected to display the same courageous and athletic skills in time of peace – in the hunting field and on the race track. Hunting was at once a diversion and a rehearsal for war. In the bas-reliefs of the ancient civilizations the rulers are portrayed not so much with their people, or presiding over their courts, or studying their books, but mostly with bow and arrow, sword and spear, in a chariot or astride a horse, either in pursuit of an enemy or of game.

The primitive tribes, seeing in Mother Nature an awe-inspiring magic, idolised her, and since hunting involved as close a dialogue with Nature as man could reach, they held their quarry in high respect and affection. In Europe their venatic rituals became more and more cloaked in pageantry, romance and chivalry, colour and music. From Roman times onwards, the Gauls, of all the races of the West, were Europe's most sporting people, as Arrian and Julius Caesar, among others, have both testified. To the medieval French the scenes witnessed in the Royal hunt were the most beautiful in the world.

In the eleventh century, the French portrayed hunting scenes on their tapestries, and when the first modern text on hunting with hounds (*chasse à courre*) was written it was as elaborately illustrated as any religious work. Completed early in the fifteenth century this was the *Livre de Chasse*, the work of Gaston, Comte de Foix, a relation of the Plantagenets and known from his good looks as Phoebus, after the sun-god Phoebus Apollo. It may be fairly claimed on behalf of those draughtsmen and painters who lent their talent so lavishly to the book that they were the first sporting artists of distinction in the western world (*see Plate 1*).

The *Livre de Chasse* was, incidentally, translated into English under the title *The Master of Game* by Edward III's grandson, Edward, Duke of York, who commanded the vanguard at Agincourt (that work being completed while York was a prisoner in Pevensey castle on a treason charge).

Until the end of the sixteenth century sport in art continued to be rather more prominent in tapestry and book illustration than upon canvas. Among those artists specialising in *chasse à courre*, falconry, fishing and shooting, during the Renaissance were the Dutch painter, Jan van Eyck (1390–1441); Lucas Cranach the Elder (1472–1553), court painter to three successive Electors of Saxony; Jorg Kölderer of Innsbruck (c1470–1540) who illustrated the *Gejaid Buch* for Carl von Spaur, master of game to that great Nimrod, the Emperor Maximilian I; and Johannes van der Straet, of Bruges (1523–1605), popularly known as Stradanus and a student of Michaelangelo. And, above all, there was Albrecht Dürer (1471–1528) of Nüremburg, a close friend of Martin Luther, an artist with a passion for natural history and another one who illustrated books for Maximilian. A master of linear design, Dürer was wonderfully free in all his

A portrait by Robert
Peake. Henry, Prince of
Wales (1594–1612) about
to administer the *coup de
grace* to a wounded fallow
deer.

drawing. He was perhaps the first of the moderns to show true accuracy in animal
anatomy; he was certainly the best exponent of his day in copper-plate
engraving.

England's school of sporting art would become the most famous of all, but
at the end of the sixteenth century she was well behind in that field. Her hunting
ceremonies derived from France as we see from the woodcuts in George Turbeville's (*c*1540–1610) *Noble Arte of Venerie*, which was directly translated, in
the 1570s, from Jacques Du Fouilloux's *Vénerie*. There Queen Elizabeth, in due
francophile ceremony, receives the stag's fewments (droppings) laid on a plate
of fresh leaves, from her master of the hunt, the character of the droppings reveal-
ing the size and age of the stag that has been harboured for her to shoot. Another
of the book's drawings shows her 'taking assay', that is to say receiving the
proferred knife in order to slit the deer's stomach for the ritual of ascertaining

the thickness of fat. The illustrations decorating the edition of Turbeville's book, which was published for the accession of James I, are precisely the same except that James replaces Elizabeth.

The cult of the horse brought a new dimension into sporting art and in particular into sporting portraiture. Holbein (c1465–1524) was not asked to portray his sitters on their favourite chargers, but Velazquez (1599–1660) and van Dyck (1599–1641) were. The reason for this was that in Europe – starting with the Hispanic riding school at Naples and spreading, in the seventeenth century, to the royal academies that made the names of Pluvinel, Reidinger, La Guerinière and Newcastle famous – the breeding of quality horses and the science of equitation had become great aristocratic preoccupations. The drawings by Abraham van Diepenbeck (?1596–1675) a pupil of Rubens, illustrating Newcastle's *General System of Horsemanship*, were sedulously studied throughout the courts of Europe, and helped, along with the oils of Velazquez, van Dyck and others to convince the princes and nobles of Europe that, when it came to portraiture, 'a fine horse' as they said, 'completes a fine gentleman'.

Born in 1592 William Cavendish, Duke of Newcastle, was friend and courtier to Charles I, whose best known portrait (by van Dyck) and statue (by Le Sueur) are both equestrian, reflecting what was described by a contemporary as 'his Majesty's delight in the use of the great Horse, whom, already dressed, no man doth more skilfully manage, or better break, if rough and furious'.

Newcastle was also the tutor (particularly equestrian) to the future Charles II, whose devotion to the turf and chase was at least as great as that of his grandfather James I, and in whose reign the first great English sporting artist emerged. He was Francis Barlow (?1626–1704) who was dubbed by Evelyn 'ye famous painter of fowls, birds and beasts'. Barlow illustrated Richard Blome's tome, *The Gentleman's Recreation* (1686), which is nearly all concerned with hunting, shooting, fishing and racing. Much of his inspiration came from Holland, from Francis Cleyn (1582–1658), Jan Fyt (1611–1661), Abraham Hondius (c1638–95) and the Haarlem painter of hunting episodes and battle scenes, Jan Wyck (1640–1700), who is also said to have painted the horses in Kneller's equestrian pictures.

The turf had become so popular in the reign of Charles II that already, by 1680, Thomas de Grey was complaining (in *The Compleat Horseman*) that 'the noble science' of high-school horsemanship was quite abandoned in favour of racing. Of the three progenitors of the English Thoroughbred, the Byerley Turk was foaled in the 1680s, the Darley Arabian about 1700 and the Godolphin Arabian in the 1720s. John Wootton (1682–1764), born when Barlow was in middle age, was the man who was first commissioned to paint them and their progeny (*see Plate 2*). By the time George I ascended the throne racing had become a large and sophisticated industry, and Wootton a rich man.

He was patronised by that avid sportsman the 3rd Duke of Beaufort who had the hall at Badminton decorated with Wootton's gigantic hunting pictures, as did Lord Spencer at Althorp and Lord Bath at Longleat. Wootton was described by a jealous contemporary as 'a cunning fellow . . . and has made a great

interest among the nobility, but he is the dirtiest painter I ever saw'. Be that
as it may, Wootton was certainly a poor anatomist. A cursory glance at such
portraits of his as *Flying Childers*, *Smiling Ball* or *The Byerley Turk*, with their
wooden lines, jutting hocks, poor gaskins and overlong cannon bones, are
enough to convince the modern eye that, if those racehorses really looked like
that, they would not only have been snail-slow but prone to every sort of
unsoundness.

James Seymour (c1702–52), who was working at the same time as Wootton,
was not only a great deal more accurate on conformation but he endowed his
animals with more vigour and movement and thus more charm, too. The third
most important of that generation of English equestrian artists was Thomas
Spencer (1700–63), who rendered many fine racehorse portraits.

Since the English landed aristocracy was now more than ever preoccupied
with the chase and the turf, the demand for portraits of horses, hounds and
hawks and for paintings of racing and hunting scenes, burgeoned, and a suc-
cession of Continental artists responded to the demand. Chief among those was
Pieter Tillemans (1684–1734), a painter and etcher from Antwerp, who arrived
in England in 1708, and became particularly well known for his Newmarket

15

A match at Newmarket Heath in 1735 by James Seymour.

scenes at the time when Queen Anne and George I and their racing manager, Tregonwell Frampton (who as early as 1695 had been appointed 'keeper of the Running Horses to his Sacred Majesty King William III'), were prominent there. Tillemans' principal patrons were the Duke of Devonshire and Lord Byron. Then there were four generations of the Bavarian Sartoriuses. John (1700–c1780), his son Francis (1734–1804), (*see Plate 2*), grandson John Nost(1759–1828) and great-grandson John Francis (*c*1775–1831). Arguably the best of these was John Nost, frequently referred to as John Nost Sartorius Jnr or J. N. Sartorius, whose work is marked by landscapes and naive figures of great charm (*see Plate 3*). John Cordrey (*c*1765–1825) painted in rather similar style.

The most prolific – and the most informative – sporting artist in the world during the first half of the eighteenth century must have been the German Johann Elias Ridinger (1698–1767). He not only specialised in the portrayal of all the field sports of those days – including stag and boar hunting, hawking, shooting,

PLATE I   (*above*) A detail from the *Livre de Chasse* by Gaston de Foix, a manuscript made in the Netherlands in the early fifteenth century.

(*right*) A discussion between two court ladies on the respective merits of hawking and hunting with hounds. From an illuminated manuscript by Guillaume Cretin, Rouen, about 1525.

PLATE 2 *Riding Party* by
John Wootton, *c* 1710.

A conversation piece by
Francis Sartorius, *c* 1787.
The portraits are of
Edward, 2nd Earl of
Aldborough and his
Countess, at Stratford
Lodge, County Wicklow.

fishing, luring and snaring – but also in predation between the animals themselves and in equestrian *haute école*. Ridinger's engravings decorated more books and more walls than those of any other man at any time.

Two of the most eminent animal and sporting artists working around that period were the Frenchman, Alexandre-Francois Desportes (1661–1743) and Jean-Baptiste Oudry (1686–1755). Desportes (who was apprenticed to a Flemish animal artist called Bernaert, who had been a pupil of Frans Snyders), first made a name for himself at the court of the Polish King Jan Sobieski II. By the start of the eighteenth century Desportes was appointed painter of the chase to Louis XIV, who was so keen to encourage him that he allowed him to attend, without hindrance, as many of the royal hunts as he wished. When Louis gave up hunting, Desportes undertook several commissions in England. Louis XV, on succeeding to his great-grandfather's throne, continued the royal patronage. Desportes won a name for impeccable accuracy in his animal likenesses, his details of the land-scape, trees and flowers, and for integrating his animals so naturally in their settings.

John Nost Sartorius: *Mr Champion out shooting with his setters*, 1797.

Both Desportes and Oudry displayed a magnificent feeling for animal sensibility. Oudry first became well known with a portrait of Peter the Great who sat for him on a visit to Paris. The artist was then, like Desportes, employed by Louis XV, who allotted him a studio in the Louvre. Perhaps his best known works were his designs for the enormous tapestries entitled *Le Chasses de Louis XV*, woven in the 1730s. The king himself supervised the work which took 13 years. But Oudry's most accomplished paintings, I think, were his portraits of the royal hounds and working dogs.

Sporting art is about nothing if it is not about anatomy and athletic movement; and although it may be fairly claimed on behalf of Desportes and Oudry that they possessed a deep knowledge of both the character and shape of the creatures they drew, neither expressed a thorough knowledge of their subjects' (either animal or human) anatomy. They virtually worked from the surface. It was left to an Englishman of a generation or two later, George Stubbs (1724–1806) to show how the breathing body, and the bone and muscle structure beneath the fur or glossy coat could be revealed three-dimensionally in oil paints.

Stubbs's lifelong passion for the study of anatomy was almost an obsession. As a small boy he begged the family doctor for bones to draw, and in his teens persuaded surgeons to let him watch when they dissected corpses or carried out operations. When requested by his drawing tutor to copy another artist's work he refused, saying 'I will look into Nature herself and copy only her!' And on that resolution abruptly abandoned the tutor.

After travelling for a while in Italy to study the Renaissance masters he returned to England and took a house in Lincolnshire so he could start work on his *Anatomy of the Horse*. Aided by a system of bars, hoists and hooks he suspended his skinned horses and horse skeletons from a ceiling, hanging a plank underneath to support the feet, and we are told that Mary Spencer (who was assumed to be his common-law wife and mother of his son, George Townley Stubbs) 'tolerated the horrible odour of putrefying flesh'.

Later on he drew the big cats in the Tower of London; he sketched the lion at Lord Shelburne's villa at Hounslow; he painted a lifesize portrait of a cheetah sent from India to the King; and once, when undressing for bed at 10 p.m., word came to him that 'a tiger has just died at Mr Pidcock's in the Strand'. Stubbs re-dressed at once, took a carriage to the menagerie and bought the carcass for 3 guineas. By daybreak he had skinned and dissected it. 'Constant labour', as Balzac said, 'is the first law of art.' From childhood to the grave it was a law never disobeyed by Stubbs.

Gossip abounded concerning his acquisition and treatment of dead models. 'A hundred times', whispered *The Sporting Magazine*, 'he ran into such adventures at night as might subject anyone with less honourable motives to the greatest severity of the law.' The naturalist and explorer Sir Joseph Banks was to receive a letter of complaint alluding to the 'vile renown' of Stubbs's anatomical practices. But others were greatly impressed by the lengths to which the artist went to achieve accuracy. Edmund Burke, exhorting his protégé James

Barry to emulate Stubbs wrote: 'Notwithstanding your natural repugnance to handling carcasses you ought to make the knife go with the pencil and study anatomy in real!'

Having completed his series of drawings and their accompanying 250,000-word text for *The Anatomy of the Horse*, Stubbs went to London to put his pictures in the hands of an engraver. Although this book was not published until 1766, sufficient influential people soon saw the etchings for word to reach the titans of the turf and hunting field that here at last was a man who could draw horses with absolute truth and each to its own character.

Stubbs could not have arrived at a more propitious time than in the 1760s to earn fame as an animal artist in England. The Royal Academy exhibitions were about to start and a period of great economic prosperity had begun. This was the age of Robert Adam and Capability Brown, and the dawn of the era in which English landowners pursued the pleasures of the countryside as among life's most serious businesses.

Charles Pelham, of Brocklesby, had started the first hound lists in the 1740s, and a decade or two later Hugo Meynell (in what is now the Quorn country) was breeding hounds fast enough to catch their foxes in the open – in the middle of the day instead of laboriously following up their drag from dawn. Thus hunters had to be flyers, too, and to be capable of jumping the fences which had been planted to satisfy the Enclosure Acts. By the 1760s, with foxhunting superseding hare and stag hunting as the leading British field sport, riding to hounds became at once the most fashionable, popular and picturesque of participant sporting activities.

George Stubbs's painting of a zebra, 1763.

A Stubbs study: *Two gentlemen out shooting at Creswell Crags, 1767.*

Also around the time Stubbs 'arrived' the flintlock had improved sufficiently to render it what was described by a contemporary as 'the first weapon fit for a sporting gentleman'. Although MacAdam and Telford did not come on the road improvement scene until towards the end of the artist's life, surfaces had already improved, carriages streamlined, draught horses and ponies smartened, and owners generally were taking much more pride in their equipages. In the middle of the eighteenth century, too, the story of prize cattle began in earnest.

The racehorse, bred more now to English and Irish mares, was beginning to move away from the Arabian character, towards the look and the speed of the modern Thoroughbred. The racing industry had grown apace since the time of Charles II; the term Thoroughbred racehorse had been in parlance since about 1710, the Jockey Club was founded in 1752, and Richard Tattersall founded his sales at Hyde Park Corner in 1766.

Racing, driving, hunting, shooting and farming all assumed a greater social importance. Grandees, such as the Dukes of Ancaster, Grafton and Portland and Lords Bolingbroke, Grosvenor, Rockingham and Torrington, whose fathers may have gone, with no consummate satisfaction, to Tillemans, Wootton and Seymour, were all looking for a man of Stubbs's genius to paint their animals and themselves. All of them were to employ him.

As a naturalist, devotee of life in the countryside and faithful portraitist of human physiognomy as well as the most realistic animal artist that ever lived – certainly more accurate in movement than Dürer – Stubbs always succeeded in integrating his true-to-life figures in true-to-life settings. He neither idealised his compositions (except in his literally romantic or allegorical studies) as many of his predecessors were prone to do; nor did he sentimentalise them as Herring and Landseer would do. At the Royal Academy annual exhibition of 1787, for example, a dramatic painting by Stubbs of bulls fighting was condemned by the critics as 'too tame'. Those critics had never seen bulls fighting; Stubbs had watched them for hours.

When he shows us women in trim, ankle-length dresses and ornate hats help-ing with the harvest, or soldiers of the 10th Light Dragoons ('Prinny's' regiment) with relaxed faces (though at positions of 'attention') we may be confident that is precisely how they looked, just as we can be sure that the huge arched crests with which he endowed Mambrino or the Godolphin Arabian were no exaggeration.

Reinagle and Gilpin were to be vaunted by many critics as the great illustrators of shooting scenes. But they are not as true as Stubbs who was himself a keen game shot and, incidentally, one of the few artists (then or later) who could, in my opinion, show the fit of a gun in the sportsman's shoulder correctly. As he told that tutor of his youth, he would not, he could not, lie.

The brisk workmanlike demeanour of Stubbs's grooms and stable boys and the humble (not servile) and often melancholy look on the faces of his labourers, contrasting with the self-assured hauteur of his patrons and their families, subtly reflected the attitudes within the social strata of the rural England of George III, as much as the clothes they wore. An eighteenth century camera would not have revealed more.

Equestrian art had to wait for photography to reveal the rhythm and action of the canter. Stubbs, attempting nothing he could not see, adhered to *ventre à terre*; yet, knowing as well as anyone the working of bones, muscles and tendons he achieved an image of levitation and impulsion that eluded other artists.

One of his finest equestrian portraits, painted at the age of 75, is that of Hambletonian (winner among many other races of the 1795 St Leger) after the last race the horse ran. Hambletonian was matched against his closest rival, Diamond, over the four mile course at Newmarket, and won the contest by a short head. But Hambletonian's jockey drove him so furiously across the last lap, and the horse was in such a state of exhaustion at the end, that his owner, Sir Henry Vane-Tempest, decided never to race him again. Stubbs shows the heaving, shuddering Thoroughbred held by his groom to be rubbed down by his stable boy straight after the race, and you can almost feel, through the pigments, the old artist sharing, pang for pang, the victor's suffering.

During his last years Stubbs was working on a sketchbook entitled *A Comparative Anatomical Exposition of the Structure of the Human Body with that of a Tiger and a Common Fowl*. It was as though his life's ambition was to gain the secret of the inter-relationship of all sentient life. At 8 a.m. on the morning of 9 July 1806, obviously close to his end, he said to his friends: 'Perhaps I am going to die; but I fear not death; I had indeed hoped to have finished my *Comparative Anatomy* ere I went, but for other things I have no anxiety'.

Eclipse, the most important sire of all time and the property of Colonel Dennis O'Kelly, was painted several times by Stubbs. This paragon (at the time the property of William Wildman) was first run in heats in 1769. After he won his first heat quite easily, O'Kelly, being unimpressed by the odds for the second, offered 'for the same sum to name the placings of the runners'. He then bellowed his immortal prophecy: 'Eclipse first, the rest nowhere!' (meaning the others would be too far behind for the judges to see how they were placed.) O'Kelly won his bet and bought Eclipse, who was never to be beaten in his life. Hence Sir Alfred Munning's parody: 'Stubbs first, the rest nowhere!' The distinguished art critic, Basil Taylor, described Stubbs as being 'next to Leonardo da Vinci the greatest painter-scientist in history'. And that is why I have dwelt for so long on that king of animal artists.

Prolific though Stubbs was he did not leave many hunting pictures behind him; yet Lionel Edwards, the best, I think, of all the hunting artists, ancient or modern, was to give the opinion that Stubbs's finest single picture was *The Grosvenor Hunt*, a 1760s scene showing the pack closing in to take their stag at the edge of a stream with the huntsman blowing his circular horn, and the Lord Grosvenor and half-a-dozen of his followers opposite. The focal point is not the Earl who commissioned the picture but the stag and the leading hounds, and all the riders are dressed in practical workaday riding clothes along with their green hunt coats.

That is in sharp contrast to the royal hunting scenes from the brushes of Desportes and Oudry in which everyone is most ornately clothed according to their rank, and all eyes are on the king. The pursuit is mainly concerned with pomp

Stubbs in melodrama: *Stallions fighting*, 1791.

and ceremony while the English equivalent concentrates on the action itself. It was largely this sport-for-sports-sake attitude in England that gave her artists so much more freedom and variety in their subject matter than their Continental counterparts and that – coupled with its stimulus, patronage – was to render British sporting art the most sought-after in the world.

Notwithstanding the critics' prejudice against sporting art and the royal and aristocratic patronage that went with those subjects – and in spite of Stubbs's preoccupation with horse and dog, gun, hawk and rod – those critics were bound to acknowledge the genius of 'Mr Stubbs the horse painter' as he was popularly known. But they would not ungrudgingly extend the same praises to his successors – bound as they were to their turfite, foxhunting, landowning patrons – however brilliant some of their work was to be. It was a matter of snobbery. It would not do for a critic to be seen or heard lauding a portrait of a foxhound, or gundog, or of Thoroughbreds lining up for the start. In particular the first President of the Royal Academy, Sir Joshua Reynolds, who favoured grand portraiture and classical and historical scenes help set the prejudice by making a

23

point of scorning sporting pictures. (Dr Johnson, as staunch an Englishman as he was a wide one, did not agree: 'I would rather see the portrait of a dog I knew well', he said, 'than all the allegories you can show me!') Yet those subjects were a good deal more difficult to handle than a landscape or still life or even a human portrait whose subject may be requested to sit still or turn this way or that.

But 'Stubbs first, the rest nowhere . . .'? There were many in the next generation or two, who, if they did not equal him, were only a few lengths behind, one or two perhaps as little as half-a-length or a short head. Let us take a look at thumbnail sketches of 16 more who were born before the eighteenth century was eclipsed. First, in order of seniority, comes Sawrey Gilpin (1733–1807). Scion of an old Cumberland family and patronised by the Duke of Cumberland (famed for his leadership against the '45 uprising) and by that fanatically keen sportsman, Colonel Thornton, of Thornville Royal, Gilpin was a very able sporting artist and one who, towards the end of his life was asked by Romney, Turner and Zoffany to add animals to their paintings.

Next comes one of Gilpin's most gifted pupils, Thomas Gooch (c1750–1802), who went on to exhibit a total of 76 paintings, mostly horses and dogs, at the Royal Academy. He is perhaps best known for his poignant series *The Life of a Racehorse*, which, in 1792, was re-issued as a folio with an essay by Dr Hawksworth, entitled *To Excite a Benevolent Conduct to the Brute Creation*. Gooch was followed by Thomas Rowlandson (1756–1827), a man of wonderful humour, celebrated for his rounded and ebullient pen-and-ink wash caricatures and hilarious racecourse scenes. Dean Wolstenholme Snr (1757–1837), a 'gentleman-artist' with no formal training, showed a splendid eye for sporting incidents; his most famous canvas was *The Epping Forest Hunt* (1811). His son, of the same name (1798–1883), displayed a similar style; *The Death of Tom Moody* was one of Dean Jnr's that became a popular print.

The output of J. C. Ibbetson (1759–1817) was small, but it was very vigorous (*see Plate 10*). Walter Shaw Sparrow made a comment on him especially interesting in the context of this book: 'A young collector of sporting sketches, and of country life interesting to sportsmen, cannot do better than place Rowlandson, and Ibbetson also, in the front line of his research, one reason being that his hobby will conduct him into many pleasant byways where he will pick up a great deal of entertaining old social history . . . Ibbetson did charming country-life pieces in watercolour; and his pastorals in oil pigment, low in tone, and easily recognised by their painter's fondness for yellow ochre have a swift and firm directness of touch . . . Sporting subjects in Ibbetson are uncommon, but much else in his work is valuable to that complete study of sport which includes vanished phases of country life and customs. This applies also to Rowlandson, as to Morland. There is more English sportsmanship in Ibbetson's rustic figure subjects and cattle pictures than in rocking-horse gallops by F. Sartorius, who never learnt how to paint . . .'

Born next, George Morland (1763–1804) was a child prodigy who first

PLATE 3   A scene in a stable yard by J. N. Sartorius Jnr, 1780

PLATE 4 *The Quorn Hunt in Full Cry near Tiptow Hill* by John Ferneley Snr, 1832. Keen foxhunter, game-shot and fisherman, Ferneley was a sportsman through and through. The Melton scenario was his heaven.

PLATE 5 *The Cur* by
John Ferneley Snr,
1848.

Gone Away! by John Ferneley Jnr, *c* 1838; Melton Mowbray features in the distance. Although
nowhere near the artistic stature of his father, the younger Ferneley painted a large number of hunting
scenes very much in the style of the great Ferneley.

exhibited at the Royal Academy at the age of 15. His rustic scenes carry enormous charm (*see Plate 6*), despite the fact that he was an alcoholic who spent a lot of time in debtors' prisons. Dying at the age of 41 he designed a skull and crossbones motif for his gravestone and wrote his own epitaph: 'Here lies a Drunken Dog'. Charles Towne (1763–1840), an early member of the Old Liverpool School, was born and brought up in Wigan in circumstances of acute poverty and began his career as a coach painter. Lack of training somewhat marred his sense of perspective and composition but he produced some very fine horse portraiture.

Ben Marshall (1768–1834) stands head and shoulders above most of the sporting artists of his era, not only because his animal likenesses were very acute, but also because his human figures and faces, so extraordinarily lifelike, reflect the character of sporting England at the turn of the eighteenth century as no others could (*see Plate 11*). His was a rather sad life: his mother died when he was four, he was crippled when a coach in which he was travelling overturned, and he died almost penniless. When Marshall's colleagues tried to persuade him not to desert London for Newmarket he lifted his hands in disagreement: 'I have good reason for going', he told them; 'I discover many a man who will pay me 50 guineas for painting his horse, who thinks 10 too much for painting his wife.' (Similarly, Reynolds once muttered disdainfully that while his full length human portraits only fetched 100 guineas, Stubbs would be paid 150 guineas for a horse). On another occasion Marshall advised a student that: 'A painter should never be satisfied. When that is the case he has done improving, and when he ceases to improve he ought to die'. Marshall counted John Ferneley and Abraham Cooper among his pupils.

James Ward (1769–1859), another of the really towering sporting artists of this period, was a deeply religious – and a rather intense and humourless – man, who was outraged when two of his sisters married fellow artists (Chalon and Morland), who deserted them. Ward started as a bottle-washer, progressing to a painter of animals in the 1780s and becoming well known for it in the '90s. In 1800 he was commissioned by the Agricultural Society to paint a series of 200 pictures illustrating the principal breeds of farm animals. His equestrian portraits are marvellously animated.

The mother of Henry Barnard Chalon (1770–1849) was the daughter of a financier, who became Lord Mayor of London and a MP, and who cut his daughter off when she married Chalon's father, the artist's most influential tutor, a Dutch musician and engraver. Chalon was a sporting painter who possessed a wonderful eye for minute detail and facility for achieving likenesses. At the age of 25 he was appointed animal artist to the Duchess of York. Nearly all his pictures exude great airs of authority.

R. B. Davis (1782–1854) was the son of Richard Davis who was huntsman to George III's pack of harriers and brother of the celebrated Charles Davis, huntsman for 44 years of the Royal Buckhounds. Having been brought up alongside hounds and horses, it is not surprising, given his talent, that he portrayed them delightfully. Davis produced a *Hunter's Annual* series of prints, depicting

John Ferneley Snr: Lord Brownlow's bull terriers, Nelson and Argo,
beside the stables at Belton House in 1831.

huntsmen with their hounds of many different packs. F. C. Turner (c1782–1846)
was another who hunted in several parts of Britain (*see Plate 10*). He is perhaps
best known for the great impression of speed he injected into his paintings.

That brings us to John Ferneley Snr (1782–1860), who was born in Leicestershire at about the same time as Davis and Turner. The 4th Duke of Rutland,
observing young Ferneley's impressive efforts, persuaded the boy's carpenter and
wheelwright father to have him apprenticed to Ben Marshall. Ferneley, keen
foxhunter, gameshot and fisherman, was a sportsman through and through; the
Melton Mowbray scenario was his heaven. He painted many pictures for
Thomas Assheton Smith, Master of the Quorn, and was patronised by several
other foxhunting grandees (*see Plate 4*). Among his other hard-riding patrons
were the Duke of Rutland and Lords Westminster, Cardigan, Cadogan, Forester,
Gardiner, Jersey, Middleton and Tyrone. Notwithstanding his artisan background he was accepted on equal terms in the hunting field by the Melton bucks.

26

Ferneley and Alken were the great artists of the hunting field in the first half of the nineteenth century. The Scottish painter, Sir Francis Grant (1803–78) who was renowned for his equestrian portraits (especially those of Queen Victoria and Prince Albert, Palmerston and Macaulay), had a style very similar to Ferneley's.

Henry Alken Snr (1785–1851), ardent foxhunter, too, was next into the world. The Alkens, Danish political refugees, had fled to England in the 1750s. They were called Seffrien, the adopted 'Alken' being their north Jutland village. It was a talented family; Henry's grandfather carved in wood and stone; his father, Samuel, was an architectural designer, etcher and aquatinter. Henry was an avidly enthusiastic horseman, who, with a sound art training behind him, went to Melton Mowbray in about 1809 and rode with the Shire packs.

Making a close study of the scenes, young Alken turned out a stream of action pictures, full of wit, gaiety, bravado and hot-blooded aristocratic hauteur. He worked under the pseudonym, 'Ben Tally Ho', causing great speculation among the Melton bloods as to his identity. In 1816 he owned up. He became celebrated as an illustrator, especially of Nimrod's books of which his illustrations for *The*

One of Henry Alken's lithographs: *A Few of the Right Sort who have done the Right Thing*, 1821–2.

27

Life of the Late John Mytton Esq are perhaps the best known. Early in middle age, despite his great success, he went into a decline, he drank and his health deteriorated rapidly. He died a broken, penniless old man in 1851. However, he leaves us a wonderfully graphic image of sporting Leicestershire at around the time – and after – that Wellington was trouncing the French.

Another of Marshall's pupils to indulge in the principal field sports was Abraham Cooper (1787–1868), who, in his turn, was to give lessons to J. F. Herring Snr and William Barraud. This masterly animal artist, who also enjoyed painting historical and classical subjects, was elected a Royal Academician in 1820. Cooper was a regular contributor to *The Sporting Magazine*. Its obituary notice described him as 'a guileless pleasant gentleman and a thorough sportsman who rode well to hounds, was a good shot and a clever fly fisherman'. Last in this gallery of 16 artists to first see the light of day in the eighteenth century after Stubbs comes the Yorkshire painter, David Dalby (1794–1836). He specialised particularly in equine portraits and coaching scenes. His touch was at once soft, sensitive and fluent and he showed great feeling for the rhythm and impulsion of horses and hounds.

Those very brief vignettes should not mislead the reader into forming the opinion that the British held almost the entire monopoly of artistic talent in the genre. As we have seen, the great era of British art could not dawn without the Flemish spark, without such wizards as Hondius, Fyt, Wyck, van Diepenbeck and Tillemans, and others from the Continent like the Bohemian Wenceslaus Hollar. Later, I mentioned the Sartorius family and the Alkens. 'It is not overmuch to say that British sport in art has owed as much to foreigners', comments Shaw Sparrow, 'as our best racehorses have owed to their descent from the Darley Arabian, the Byerley Turk and the Godolphin Arabian'.

The Flemish animal and sporting artists found their principal patrons in France before Louis XIV ascended the throne. In the late seventeenth century and during the eighteenth century, when the spotlight of French field sports was focused on the court at Versailles, and afterwards, when the Monarchy was broken, many Continental artists flocked to England to seek work under the aegis of the growing number of patrons who wanted their dogs and racehorses, hunting establishments and triumphs on the turf, prize cattle, favourite hunters and themselves with rod or gun depicted for posterity. There was Jacques-Laurent Agasse (1767–1849), a Swiss and a pupil of David, who settled in England in 1800 and was patronised by that great breeder of horses, Lord Rivers. Agasse is represented here (*Plate 7*) with a most sensitive and engaging study of foxhounds. And there was Jean-Louis-André Théodore Gericault (1791–1824), a pupil of Vernet and Guerin, celebrated for both his military and sporting scenes; Eugène Delacroix (1798–1863) and Alfred de Dreux (1810–60).

The English squires wished their portraits to reflect their power of ownership. The musket they held, the retriever that fawned at their knees, the hounds that gazed adoringly at them from around their horses' feet, were all symbols of their privilege and material potency; for they, and they alone were permitted

The Shooting Pony. An 1825 painting by Abraham Cooper.

to pursue the quarry across their broad acres. (The Game Laws saw to that).
The horse that so many bestrode for their sittings personified their superior position vis-à-vis their tenants and servants. The successful racehorse – grouped,
perhaps, with jockey, trainer and stable lad – and prize bull or champion hound,
copied onto canvas by a Marshall, a Ferneley or a Ward, rendered prestige among
those grandees' peers.

The artists could scarcely keep pace with their commissions, because sport
had now assumed an unprecedented importance in Britain. The racecourses had
burgeoned and the activities of the turf had become highly sophisticated.
Steeplechasing, born from the union of flat racing and foxhunting was on the
way in and, said Nimrod, 'men rode as if spare necks were to be had as easily
as spare stirrup leathers'. Alken's *Moonlight Steeplechase* series evoked the

29

Cropped and Nicked – Mr Richard Smith on his Hackney crossing Barnersbury Common by James Pollard, 1828.

amateur riders' wild and abandoned spirit. In the hunting field an increasing number of squires were converting from hare to fox and with more followers and more scarlet coats and larger packs of hounds producing more sensational scenes for the painter. In the Shires, Alken (again) fostered social ambition with his set entitled *Doing the Thing*.

After Macadam and Telford had progressed well with their work of surfacing the roads with granite and other durable stones, broken small enough to give roads and tracks a hard and relatively smooth surface, more people indulged in coaching for pleasure, while the turnout of equipages and horses was of increasing importance.

'It is the horse's animal beauty and power, which most thrilled the coach traveller', wrote De Quincey in his *English Mail Coach*: 'we heard our speed, we felt it as thrilling; and this speed was incarnated in the fiery eyeballs of the noblest among brutes, in his dilated nostrils, spasmodic muscles and thunder beating hooves'. James Pollard (1792–1867) who was in his prime during the great coaching era, was the artist who specialised principally in those driving scenes which have become so popular with collectors in our own day (*see Plate*

30

8). Charles Cooper Henderson (1803–77) came very close to him in that field (Pollard was also a prolific illustrator of the field sports.) Long-distance driving was killed off by the railways, however, and within half a century of that, most other horse-drawn conveyance was eclipsed by the motorcar.

Falconry waned as the shotgun improved, but with the innovation of breech-loading and the preservation of game – which, between them, led the game-shot away from walking up birds to having them driven towards him – the shooting scene became less picturesque. There were fine shooting pictures from the brushes of Stubbs, Reinagle, Cooper, William Jones, Richard Ansdell and others, but their successors found more delight in other country pursuits. Coursing became more fashionable following Lord Sefton's foundation of the Altcar Club in 1825 and the start of the Waterloo Cup a decade later, which led to further commissions for the good action animal artist. Fishing subjects came more from artists' whims and fancies than from commissions. Morland, Pollard (*see Plate 9*), Cooper, Jones and Frederick Lewis (*see Plate 21*) were among those who found enjoyment in the angling scene.

The old dividing lines between social ranks were beginning to blur. The Industrial Revolution paved the way for a broader-based society. More people, the expanding middle class, were hunting, fishing, shooting, driving and racing (often as owners); more took an interest in those subjects in art. The eighteenth century was the age of the great landowners; in the nineteenth the small land-owner was creeping in. Women, too, were indulging increasingly in sport – archery, croquet, fishing and even, at last, foxhunting. The popularity of sporting art was reflected in a burgeoning of prints. Surtees tells us, for instance, that

Pheasant Shooting by A. S. Boult, *c*1850.

31

in Jorrocks's house hung 'a coloured copy of John Warde on Blue Ruin, while Mr Ralph Lambton on his horse, Undertaker, with his hounds and men occupied a frame on the opposite wall'.

Talking of Surtees, his friend and first illustrator, John Leech (1817–64), earned a very special place in the realm of sporting art. His drawings carry a most expressive quality, his cartoons a delightful wit, his paintings – after much coaxing by Millais to become a watercolourist – a most pleasing colour harmony. Like Alken, Leech had a tremendous feeling for dramatic (and humorous) action. He illustrated more than 50 books, including *Punch's Almanack* and much of Dickens, while his pictures appeared every week in *The Field* and *Illustrated London News*.

It was Leech who Thackeray (with whom he was at Charterhouse) 'loved most dearly of all'; it was Leech again who du Maurier described as 'the King of Impressionists; of whom the critic P. G. Hammerton, wrote 'he is comparable in power to the great serious Masters'; of whom Landseer said that 'there is hardly a sketch of his unworthy of being framed to decorate a wall'; and of whose drawings Ruskin remarked: 'In flexibility and lightness of pencilling nothing but the best outlines of the Italian masterpieces with the silver-point can be compared to them . . .' Whyte Melville spoke of 'Leech's inimitable hunting pictures'. As Leech's many letters to his best friend, Charles Adams, show, he adored his hunting. ('Oh I can imagine *nothing* more delightful than a few first-rate hunters' – to quote one of them – 'and a little first-rate pluck, and to be set going over the grass again. Is the horse I had before still alive I wonder? . . .')

The collector will frequently come across equestrian paintings by the Barraud brothers, William (1810–50) and Henry (1811–74), both of whom turned out portraits and landscapes of singular strength. William, a pupil of Abraham Cooper – and of rather greater talent, I think, than his brother – was eclipsed too soon, dying in his fortieth year.

Like Pollard, J. F. Herring Snr (1795–1865) though born in the 1790s, is not included in my post Stubbs/pre 1800 gallery, for both were early Victorians. Herring was from a family of Dutch-American expatriates. As he spent seven years of his youth driving the London to Doncaster coach, there was little he did not know about horses and the roadside scene. Enormously prolific, among hundreds of other sporting paintings he depicted 18 Derby winners, 34 successive winners of the St Leger and 11 of the Oaks. His preoccupation with blacksmith's shops and forges and farmyard scenes belong more to the autumn of his life. (*See Plates 19 and 20*). Herring's portraits of jockeys are particularly impressive. Nearly 400 of his paintings were engraved.

His contemporaries regarded him as the greatest sporting artist of the age, and although later critics have been inclined to condemn him as often too 'sweet', too sentimental, he must rank among the top half-dozen British animal artists of all time. 'Whether we put Herring above or below Ben Marshall', wrote the former's biographer, Oliver Beckett; 'whether we prefer the brilliant actuality

PLATE 6   *Casting for a scent*. One of a pair by
George Morland, *c* 1800.

PLATE 7   (*right*) A study of foxhounds by the Swiss painter, Jacques-Laurent Agasse, 1837.
A close student of anatomy and pupil of David, Agasse settled in England in 1800, being patronised principally by the great breeder of horses, Lord Rivers.

(*below*) A huntsman with hounds on the edge of a wood, by Henry Alken Jnr, *c* 1850.

of his Thoroughbreds stripped for action to all the musical metaphors adduced in favour of Stubbs's compositions; or whether the hunting man will always admire Ferneley's Quorn more than Herring's East Suffolk hunt pictures, is a matter of taste. What is sure is that the owner who sold a Herring for £68 in 1947 that came up for sale years later at £24,000, has lived to regret it'.

Of Herring's eight children, three of the boys, J.F. Jnr (1820–1907), Charles (1828–56) and Benjamin (1830–71) followed in their father's footsteps. Charles, the favourite son, proved very gifted and might have approached his father's stature as an artist had he not died at the early age of 28.

Sentimentality in animal (as in other) art was much indulged by the Victorians; but mawkish anthropomorphism was, if anything, less of a characteristic of Herring Snr than of his contemporary (and his favourite artist) Sir Edwin Landseer (1802–73), a man who came from a family of engravers and grew to be the most popular portrayer of animals in the western world in the mid-nineteenth century. His most celebrated work was that of the Trafalgar Square lions, while among his best known paintings were *Dogs of St Gothard discovering a Traveller in the Snow* (1820), *Dignity and Impudence* (1839) and *The Monarch of the Glen* (1851). Landseer, another child prodigy (he was sketching cows and horses with considerable perception at the age of six) was elected a Royal Academician in 1831 and went on to enjoy great vogue with Queen Victoria and Prince Albert.

Although Landseer exercised a good deal of influence on sporting art he himself only painted one great sporting picture, a portrait of Lord Zetland's horse

Windsor Castle in Modern Times by Sir Edwin Landseer. Commissioned by Queen Victoria in 1842.

33

Voltigeur, winner of the 1850 Derby and St Leger. Shaw Sparrow places William Huggins (1820–84) very close to Landseer and relates how, when someone told Huggins that one of his pictures was equal to a Landseer, the affronted Liverpool animal artist exclaimed: 'Landseer? If I'd had that man through my hands for six months I could have made a man of him!' Shaw Sparrow thought that Huggins's beasts of prey had 'a perception truer in natural history than that which Stubbs and Landseer gradually acquired; and when he draws them with chalks and pencils, frequently on grey paper and often slightly touched here and there with watercolour, it would be hard to find his superior'. J. G. Millais, son of the Pre-Raphaelite and President of the Royal Academy, himself a considerable wildlife and sporting illustrator, expressed strong views concerning Landseer's anatomical inaccuracies and lack of natural history knowledge. Millais held the opinion that the German Joseph Wolf (c1817–99) was 'the greatest Master of animal life that ever lived'.

This is, perhaps, an appropriate moment in which to pay tribute to Edward Troye (1808–74), a Swiss who was educated in London and, in 1831, emigrated to America to become the great artist-chronicler of that nation's Thoroughbred. Troye wrote and illustrated the *The Racehorses of America*.

The editor of a prominent New York weekly magazine, *The Spirit of the*

An 1884 study by E. A. S. Douglas of foxhounds and a terrier.

34

Times went so far as to say, in 1842: 'The extraordinary success of Mr Troye as an animal painter has brought into the field several competitors. But until experience and study joined to a good eye for the points of a horse and familiar acquaintance with his anatomy shall give them more freedom of touch and more aptitude for the details which make up a faithful likeness, Troye will be unapproachable. He is the only animal painter in this country who is thoroughly master of his art; and the facility with which he gets off the precise color of an animal, is one of his most striking characteristics. In our opinion Troye has no equal in the country and no superior in Europe'.

The late Victorian and the Edwardian periods claim their share of formidable animal artists. Randolph Caldecott (1846–86) modelled and drew with remarkable skill as a child, but he was a bank clerk for five years before attending the Manchester City School of Art, then proceeding to seek an artist's career in London. Equipped with a wonderful sense of the ridiculous, and influenced both by John Leech and John Tenniel, Caldecott was first and foremost a book illustrator. He provided pictures for nearly 60 volumes including new editions of *Aesop's Fables*, *Sing a Song for Sixpence* and other collections of stories and verses for children. He plied his trade mostly in London, but with magical boyhood memories of hunting, fishing and rambling, he always longed for the countryside.

In the opinion of his mentor and biographer, Henry Blackburn, editor of *The London Society*, Caldecott possessed 'a mastery of animal form and a power in reserve of an unusual kind . . . Amongst the most ambitious and interesting of his drawings . . . were his hunting and shooting friezes'. Caldecott certainly produced some wonderfully fluent equestrian bas-reliefs. (See, if you can, the exquisite *Horse Fair in Brittany*, or, anyhow, a colour reproduction of it). He and his wife went to the United States for his health's sake in 1886, and, while travelling down the eastern seaboard, he drew some amusing foxhunting scenes. But that October he died in Florida of acute gastritis.

The work of the Northumberland watercolourist, Joseph Crawhall (1861–1913) probably evinces a truer understanding of animal impulse, sensitivity and physiognomy than most of the genre whose dates span the two centuries. His career began as a student in Paris in the early 1880s under Aime-Morot, and continued in Tangier, where he showed himself to be a very able horseman. (He rode the winner of the Tangier Hunt Cup four years running). Some of his best work is in the Burrell Collection in Glasgow. The other hallmarks of Crawhall's drawings and paintings were unusually striking composition, economy of line and an animation that always evokes the excitement and drama of the occasion. But his output of sporting pictures was small compared with that of his great friend and admirer, the Scottish artist, G. D. Armour (1864–1949).

Although enormously prolific and successful as an artist, George Denholm Armour was firstly a sportsman. He was a fisherman, stalker, game-shot, race rider, polo player and – above all – foxhunter. ('Nothing affords action and

An example of G. D. Armour's humour, 1929: '*A' stands for Ass, as all of us know: Most hunts have a few, some a dozen or so!*.

gaiety more readily and unexpectedly than the hunting field', he said in his capacity as an artist). Following education at a Fife boarding school and the Royal Scottish Academy of Life School, he went, aged 21, to Morocco (because he 'heard a horse could be kept there for something under a shilling a day . . . This awakened in me a hitherto unrealised craving for the animal'). He became a whipper-in to the Tangier Hunt in duo with Crawhall, whom he described as 'the best animal painter of his time'. Like Caldecott, Armour was deeply influenced by Leech.

In 1911, as illustrator and writer on behalf of *Country Life*, he crossed the Atlantic to cover polo's Anglo-American Westchester Cup series of that year and combined the roles with a most impressive double insight. Along with other equestrian artists of his generation, he became a remounts officer during the

36

First World War, rising to the rank of lieutenant-colonel in Salonika. Armour had a great gift for achieving human, as well as animal, likenesses.

Lynwood Palmer (1868–1939) ran away from home to escape the conventional career demanded by his parents, travelling to America for his art apprenticeship. Almost from the moment he returned to England, in 1899, he earned his living as a horse portraitist, achieving wonderful equine likenesses, usually on very large canvases. Of the remainder of that generation, Thomas Blinks (1853–1910) and Heywood Hardy (1843–1933) though no geniuses, were perhaps the most evocative of the 1890s and turn of the century hunting field scenes.

In my opinion the greatest single horse artist of the Edwardian era, was Emil Adam (c1843–1907).

Cecil Aldin (1870–1935) seems to us essentially a twentieth century man, yet he was already 30 by 1900. A compulsive dog and horse artist from earliest childhood he was educated at Kensington's National Art Training School and then under that king of animal art teachers, Frank Calderon. A territorial remount training officer before the war he went on to command a remount training depot during it (and, incidentally, had it staffed entirely with women). Post-war he was a point-to-point rider, first hon. secretary, then joint-Master of the South Berks foxhounds, acting Master of the Walhampton bassets, and a pioneer organiser of children's gymkhanas.

Aldin was a great comic draughtsman and illustrated books by Dickens, Surtees, Kipling and Masefield. He was, above all, one of the most perceptive dog artists that ever lived. After his death the animal and sporting writer, William Fawcett, wrote that 'probably no painter of today, or yesterday, ever quite caught the soul of dogdom as Cecil Aldin did' while his obituary in *The Times* went so far as to say that 'except for John Leech, Henry Alken had no legitimate successor worthy of the name until, nearing the end of the last century, Denholm Armour and Aldin burst upon us'.

The French school, known as *Les Animaliers*, which dates roughly from the 1830s, until the turn of the nineteenth century, continually emphasised the third dimension and thus exerted considerable influence on the sporting artist (*see Plate 16*). So of course, from about the 1860s did the French Impressionists, whose free linear economy and new uses of the play of light and atmospheric effects would help to make, for example, such a difference in character between the paintings of Landseer and those of A. J. (Sir Alfred) Munnings, (1878–1959), to whom we now turn.

Munnings was a man who loved horses as warmly as Aldin loved dogs, but who painted on a much grander and more inspired scale. Having studied art at Norwich and Paris, he was first hung in the Royal Academy in 1899. Although he displayed a first-class sense of comparative anatomy, Munnings's horses are inclined to be impressionistic – more dish-faced, slender-legged, bent at the poll, tapered at the nose – and carrying smaller and more daintly pricked ears – than Nature gave them. He was supremely good at conveying light effects. He reserved the greatest admiration for the old masters, but forsook their realistic, trans-

An early Munnings watercolour: *Captain A. S. M. Summers, 19th Hussars, on Cossack*, 1909.

lucent way with paints in favour of an opaque impressionistic method of conveying colour harmonies. His horses' coats, for example, picking up the reflected colours of the sky and surroundings, accentuate their vigour and alertness. With his techniques of colour and light he has also been acclaimed as one of the greatest landscapists of the twentieth century (*see Plates 12 and 17*).

Yet Munnings was to declare himself the enemy of modern art, and could not have made the point more bluntly and abrasively than he did during his presidential speech at the 1949 Royal Academy dinner. (In 1944 he had beaten Augustus John by 24 votes to 17, in the second ballot, to become president in March, 1944, and was knighted three months later). As Sir Gerald Kelly wrote for Munnings's entry in the *Dictionary of National Biography*: 'His hostility towards the whole modern movement made him unable to believe that any sincere artist could think differently from himself'. Students of sporting art should not fail to read his autobiographical trilogy, *An Artist's Life*, *The Second Burst* and *The Finish*. He was virtually leader of the field of British sporting art from the Edwardian era until, in my view, Lionel Edwards assumed that place around the late 1920s.

38

Born in the same year as Munnings and brought up in North Wales (in the Flint and Denbigh country) Lionel Dalhousie Edwards (1878–1966) fulfilled his most important apprenticeship, like Aldin, under Calderon, and followed Aldin to membership of the London Sketch Club. He soon made a name for himself as a landscapist, as well as a portrayer of all the country sports, and became renowned for his attractively dramatic skies, which were to draw the attention of a poet laureate (John Betjeman referred in one of his verses to 'a Lionel Edwards sky'). He was, too, a prolific illustrator of books, 25 of his own and about 70 of other authors. In 1938 he composed the illustrations for R. C. Lyle's *The Aga Khan's Horses*, in which such names as Bahram, Friar's Daughter, Mumtaz Mahal, Teresina, Dastur and Mahmoud recalls some of the great events of the Turf during the 1930s. His rendering of Golden Miller, aged 23, in 1950, was regarded by the Turf pundits as one of the cleverest of all racehorse portraits.

But the first love of Edwards's life was hunting, and he is now generally upheld

A later Munnings: *Two Busvines and a Cutaway*, c1927.

39

With Lionel Edwards in the Shires in 1924: *The Belvoir. In the Vale near Jericho Gorse.*

as the greatest hunting artist of all time. It was said of him that 'his hunting pictures held the heart of England'. The equestrian writer 'Crascredo' echoed the verdicts of sportsmen everywhere after leaving a 1920s exhibition: 'It is the special triumph of Mr Lionel Edwards that in all his painting and drawing not only does he show us the truth, but mankind itself instantly knows it to be true'. After his death plaudits were showered on Edwards from every side. 'He . . . immortalised the foxhunting scenes and personalities as no other artist has done before or since', (Daphne Moore, the hound expert); 'We are indeed fortunate that a man with such a wonderful eye for landscape has been able to capture for us the atmosphere of the hunt countries', (Hon. Aylmer Tryon, founder of the Tryon Gallery and Edwards's later agent); 'His outstanding ability was for the recreation of the exciting atmosphere of the hunt', (his *Times* obituary). And so on.

Let us return, however, to the early 1900s when Edwards was first making a living as a hunting artist. For sporting art is firstly about anatomical accuracy and animal action and that was the time when he, Aldin, Munnings, Armour and others were first experimenting with ways of coming to terms with what the camera was demonstrating about action. Between the 1820s and 1880s the

40

photographic pioneers, such as Louis Daguerre, and the Nièpces and Henry Fox Talbot had been showing increasingly sophisticated images with their photographic equipment, while the public became more critical of artists' inaccuracy in conformation. ('Photography', said Shaw Sparrow, 'has done one useful thing by showing coldly, in profile portraits, the correct proportion between every racer's head and body. Till the camera became a decisive critic in this particular, scarcely a painter dared to make the head important enough. Some of Marshall's racehorses and hunters have heads ridiculously small, but his clients had other

An earlier Edwards:
The Conversation, c1925.

41

views, and were very well pleased. Herring is another expert whose horses' heads are often too short.')

Around 1880 a young American student of zoopraxography, Eadweard J. Muybridge, was attempting to capture images of rapid animal movement with his camera, and, in 1881, showing the world how successful he was, put on a display of cantering horse photographs. Yet, 20 years later, sporting artists like Armour and Aldin were still drawing the rocking horse gallop. The reason was that those photographs translated into art would not only have looked ugly to the contemporary beholder – to whom *ventre à terre* was still the height of elegance – but, to eyes thus conditioned, such a jumble of legs would not have projected a true image of speed. Lionel Edwards, who wrote an excellent essay on the subject in his autobiography, said: 'My own feeling is that to give the impression of movement requires a lot of wangling! For example, if you can lose one foot in long grass, dust, snow, or in the background shadows . . . you have already helped the illusion of speed' (*see Plate 18*).

There is only one artist who could truly have claimed to have trained under Lionel Edwards and that was Peter Biegel (1913–1987). He studied at Lucy Kemp Welch's studio at Bushey in the late 1930s, was invalided from the Army after being wounded in the D-Day landings and then resumed his studies at the Bournemouth School of Art. It was a chance meeting with the maestro on a train that led him to the studio of Lionel Edwards, whose own method and approach to his sporting art clearly rubbed off on the student. Apart from showing an outstanding facility for conveying images of racing and hunting scenes in a very clear, elegant and convincing way, Biegel was, I believe, the only man since Edwards who has managed to capture the true conformation and spirit of hounds.

In Edwards's opinion (writing in the 1940s), 'Gilbert Holiday was almost the first artist to master the photographic action, which we have become so accustomed to seeing in the daily and weekly press. By this I mean animals in motion as seen by the camera and not the artist's entirely conventional rendering, with which our immediate forefathers were perfectly satisfied . . .' While I agree with those admirers of Edwards whom I have quoted, I believe that Holiday (1879–1937) has the edge as a horse artist. He captured many subtle movements and attitudes that eluded other equine draughtsmen. 'Snaffles' paid him this tribute: 'How wonderfully Gilbert Holiday's horses are represented, their ears and eyes so full of expression and movement, their body muscles heaving under skins in the pink of condition, and their legs and feet working with a perfect natural timing as they swing along at either a gallop or trot'.

As for 'Snaffles' – Charles Johnson Payne (1884–1967) – himself, it is doubtful whether any keen British or Irish foxhunter, or steeplechaser (over the age of 50 anyway), could ever lose a mental image of those evocative crayon sketches and watercolours that appeared between the end of the Edwardian era and the beginning of the second Elizabethan era, and were printed in their thousands under such titles as *The Gent with the 'Osses to Sell*, *The Whissendine Brook*

A typical Irish hunting scene from the brushes of 'Snaffles', 1931.

*runs Deep and Wide, The Finest View in Europe, The Worst View in Europe
(Oh Murther, the dhrink ran out on me the Wrong Side of Beecher's), The Tim-
ber Merchant, The One to carry My Half-crown, 'Andsome is wot 'Andsome
does* and *The Right Man on the Wrong 'Oss.*

'Snaffles' had wonderfully poignant, amusing and generally evocative ways
of depicting sporting scenes. His racecourse, pigsticking, polo and hunting watercolours and crayon pictures, with their corner vignettes, rugged heroes, devil-
may-care heroines and no-nonsense horses, were a byword in sporting circles.

As this essay pretends to be nothing more than an introduction to the subject
of collecting sporting art, there is no room for all the talent of the generation
of Munnings and Edwards. However, another formidable artist of those days,
who I feel must be mentioned, is Alfred Grenfell Haigh (1870–1963). He worked
at Newmarket in the early years of the century, depicting racehorses exactly
as he saw them, 'warts and all', and, although he was a magnificent animal
portraitist, was not always thanked for the results. Between 1907–09 he pursued
the same role in India.

Haigh was adjutant of the Lanarkshire Yeomanry during the First World War
and, taking up his brushes again after it, continued painting until he died at
93. He was a gifted human portraitist as well as having a talent for equine and
canine likenesses; so, in addition to a huge number of racehorse paintings, he

43

Ireland's Best by Peter Curling, 1986.

received a ceaseless torrent of commissions to paint famous venatic names – Northumberland, Leconfield, Straker, Nutting, Inge, Talbot-Ponsonby, Wiggin, Fuller, Holliday, etc., – astride their favourite hunters.

Up to the Second World War there was great scope for sporting artists such as Armour, Edwards, Aldin, Holiday, Haigh and 'Snaffles' in the many glossies – the *Field*, *Bystander*, *Sphere*, *Tatler*, *Country Life* and *Illustrated London News* – whose editors regularly commissioned drawings and paintings to support equestrian, wildlife and sporting articles. As photography became easier and of better quality, however, that sideline faded. It has been much the same story with books. Contemporary sporting artists are more dependent on the galleries that patronise them and the clients who want their pictures framed on their walls.

Since the Second World War a new consciousness about, and compassion towards, animals has arisen, while field sports have been closely linked to the wildlife conservation movement. All that is prominently reflected in the work of the modern sporting artists. So who are they?

J. G. Millais' son, Raoul (b.1901) who attended the Royal Academy Schools in the early 1920s and went on to make a very well deserved name for himself as an equestrian portraitist, is still going strong. But perhaps John Skeaping (1901–80) best bridges the gap between Lionel Edwards's generation and the present one. Another infant prodigy, Skeaping was studying art full time from the age of 13, won a Royal Academy Gold Medal Travelling Scholarship at 19 and the *Prix de Rome* at 23. The letters RA followed his name from 1961 and he was Professor of Sculpture at the Royal Academy of Arts in 1964.

Though a sculptor first, Skeaping was equally at home in watercolours, gouache and pastels and specialised in the depiction of racehorses. His bronzes illustrate his considerable gift for bringing out a Thoroughbred's loose-limbed air of quality, while his drawing of horses in motion, distinguished by a remarkable economy of line, succeed in evoking as good an impression of speed and athleticism as any other artist has ever achieved.

When Skeaping was 70 he took on a student of 19 called Peter Curling who had spent the previous three years as a pupil in Florence of the highly regarded teacher, Signorina Simi (under whom Annigoni trained). Besides riding exercise from racing stables, Peter Curling spends much time both behind the scenes on

Offside Forehander by Ian Ribbons.

the Turf and on the racecourse. Those experiences are incisively reflected in this young artist's paintings which distil the hurly-burly of races with great realism (*see Plate 13*). He lives in Ireland and has been trying his hand, with some success, at hunting scenes. Six years older than Curling, Philip Blacker, the son of the equestrian General Sir Cecil ('Monkey') Blacker, was a professional jockey with several winners to his name before he took up equine sculpture. He pursued it with consummate success, of which one mark was his being commissioned to model a bronze trophy for the Grand National winner.

Without any doubt Susan Crawford (b.1941), another student of Signorina Simi's, is one of the world's two or three finest horse artists. She has been commissioned to paint no fewer than ten Derby winners, along with many other race-horse studies, not to mention portraits of the Queen and four other members of the Royal Family. She is rivalled quite closely by Susie Whitcombe (b.1957), an equestrian artist who has had an impressive go, among many other things, at polo scenes. Some might say that Joan Wanklyn, who is best known for her horse soldiers (in particular King's Troop Royal Horse Artillery studies), is number one today when it comes to the horse in action. It is interesting to note that, whereas equestrian art was almost entirely a male preserve until the 1960s, there are now appreciably more women involved.

The Yorkshireman Brian Rawling (b.1928), a wildlife conservationist with an excellent eye for sporting moorland, is in the lead when the subject is stalking or grouse shooting; while Rodger McPhail (b.1953), illustrator of two best-selling autobiographical books, Lord Home's *Border Reflections* and the Hon. Aylmer Tyron's *Kingfisher Mill*, gives most pleasure with fishing pictures and other branches of game shooting (*see Plate 15*). William Garfit is another who shows a strong feel for the river and the fisherman. When it comes to falconry few can beat that highly sensitive wildlife artist, Mary-Clare Critchley-Salmonson (*see Plate 14*).

Sporting art seems to be just as prone to be sniffed at by the critics now as it was in Ferneley's time. Yet, in general, today's sporting painter and sculptor demonstrates at least as much talent as his and her contemporaries working on other subjects. What is more, sporting art seems to enjoy the greater patronage, just as it did in the eighteenth and nineteenth centuries. The standards stay high and the market thrives.

2

A DEALER'S VIEWPOINT, I
SEVENTEENTH, EIGHTEENTH AND NINETEENTH CENTURIES

DAVID FULLER

Preoccupied throughout his life with the sea and with boats,
David Fuller spent his holidays from Forest School sailing along
Britain's east coast. He joined the Royal Naval Volunteer Reserve and completed
his National Service in the Navy. After a brief period as a Lloyds broker
he joined the animal and sporting art dealers, Ackermann's, in 1958.
Seven years later he became a director, and has been joint Managing Director
since 1985. He was the organiser, in 1983, of the firm's highly successful
bicentenary exhibition. He is a regular contributor of articles on
sporting art, and is now working on a definitive catalogue of
the work of Ben Marshall.

The Bower Family setting off for the Meet by H. B. Chalon, 1824.

Although other countries have produced sporting artists it is only in Britain that there developed a school of such painters. The Englishman's love for his animals and his attachment to the country life and its sport led naturally to a wish to record the choicest moments on canvas or panel. That this view is one peculiar to Britain is repeatedly demonstrated by the attitude of the foreign visitor. In the eighteenth century Le Blanc, a Frenchman, bemoaned that 'the English have no taste in the arts, preferring to hang a picture of a victorious racehorse above all other more edifying subjects', while only the other day a Japanese visitor expressed amazement that any gallery could make a living specialising in the sale of sporting art. These views did not, however, prevent many Continental artists emigrating to England to meet the ever increasing demand for sporting paintings. For, at first, there were few native born artists.

The Duke of Newcastle had employed Abraham van Diepenbeck to illustrate his great work on equitation first published in 1658 and early horse portraits at Welbeck are mainly by Continental artists. It was not, however, until after the Commonwealth (1649–60), during which the attitude to art was as a contemporary said, 'as about unfriendly as the devil towards holy water', that sporting art blossomed. This was first apparent in the work of Francis Barlow, who, although apprenticed to a portrait painter, found his real talents lay in the depiction of animals and birds.

While on the Continent the aristocracy and gentry would decorate their entrance halls with religious or mythological subjects the British chose to make their initial impact with sporting scenes. In 1681 John Evelyn, dining with his neighbour Denzil Onslow at Pyrford, recorded 'the hall was adorned with paintings of fowls and huntings, etc., the work of Mr Barlow who is excellent in this kind from the life'. These same paintings can still be seen in the Onslow seat, Clandon Park, near Guildford, now in the property of the National Trust.

The tradition continued into the next century and in the 1730s three of the major houses, Althorp, Badminton and Longleat, all had their entrance halls decorated with vast canvases by John Wootton. That this idea of decoration was not confined to the grander families is demonstrated by the survival of the painted room at Old Wilsley in Kent. It can be dated to around 1680; the upper panels show biblical scenes but the lower panels show a pack of harriers in full cry with the hare beautifully depicted on the door.

This fashion of hanging sporting paintings in country houses was now established and continued throughout the eighteenth and nineteenth centuries. In no way, however, could this be called collecting in the modern sense of the word. These pictures were simply part of the history of the family and their place was

A painting by Francis Sartorius: *Racer at Highflyer Hall, Ely, c1791*.
Having been a winner several times at Newmarket in 1782, Racer broke down
in 1783 and was then put to stud.

as natural as the dogs on the hearth or the horses in the stables, part of the
environment of the English gentleman, quietly enjoyed and appreciated by their
owners. It was only towards the end of the last century that such paintings began
to be collected by admirers with no historical family connections. Thus the collecting of sporting art as we know it today is just about one hundred years old.

This new appreciation was led by Walter Gilbey, the major part of whose
collection of over 1,000 works was housed at Elsenham Hall, in Essex. His enthusiasm resulted in his publishing not only the first book on George Stubbs but
three volumes of biographical details of sporting artists, also, issued between
1900 and 1911. Gilbey was one of the prime movers for the first exhibition of
sporting art held at the Grosvenor Gallery in 1890 whose aim was to show 'how
sport and art have always been intimately connected, and how many great men
have given their best work towards illustrating the various features of animal

50

life, and of scenery, which are beloved of the hunter and the fisherman'.

This large exhibition not only included 387 paintings and drawings but also 148 big game trophies; 107 guns and accessories; 53 silver cups and trophies and 28 sculptures. Not restricted to the British School the paintings included works by Cranach, Dürer, Snyders, Weenix, Hondecoeter, Rubens, Fyt, van der Meulen, Desportes, Velazquez, Jan Brueghel and Courbet. The English examples were led by 13 Stubbs but there was only one Marshall. Otherwise most of the major artists were represented with, naturally for the time, Landseer very much in evidence. Regretfully, the catalogue is barely more than a list of artists and titles with no sizes or provenance given, although the lender's name is prominently printed with each entry, with Gilbey himself lending over 40 paintings.

From the turn of the century until the Wall Street crash collecting sporting art became increasingly popular both in Britain and in the USA. It was during

Stubbs's portrait of the champion racehorse and sire, Dungannon, with his companion sheep. From a stipple engraving by G. T. Stubbs.

51

A fine example of equine portraiture by John Ferneley Snr: *Captain Horatio Ross's Clinker held by a groom*, 1830.

this period that Walter Shaw Sparrow published his two volumes on the subject in 1922 and 1931. These books are still required reading, and, although subsequent knowledge has revealed many errors, the breadth of original research is staggering and the illustrations copious.

The buyers were, however, still collectors with sporting interests and the paintings were judged on the merit of the subject rather than on any aesthetic principle. For instance, J. N. Sartorius was in as much demand as Stubbs. The former's *Foxhunter with Rider*, dated 1800, fetched £3,150 in 1928, whereas Stubbs's *Groom with Two Hunters* only realised £1,180 when sold at Sotheby's in 1927.

The public collections still continued to ignore sporting art, refusing to accept it as anything more than an extension of the hunting field. Undismayed by this attitude, however, such great collections as the Woolavington and Arthurton were formed in Britain and by Ambrose Clark and Theriot in the USA.

The collapse of the market after the Wall Street crash is well demonstrated by comparing the price of £750 for Stubbs's *Sir John Ramsden's Horse &*

Grooms at Sotheby's, in 1932, with *Eclipse* sold by Walter Raphael, in 1929, for £7,350. This lack of interest and money was due to continue into the Second World War when in 1940 Stubbs's *Partridge Shooting* (on porcelain) fetched £420, and two years later his *Harvesters* (also on porcelain) only struggled to £577.10.0 at Christie's. Other sporting artists were similarly affected; Ferneley's *Haworth Hounds* only made £700 at Sotheby's in 1931, whereas his *Belvoir Hunt* had reached £3,100 in the same saleroom in 1928.

Of course it was not only sporting art that collapsed, and it is often forgotten that total sales at Christie's did not exceed their 1929 level until 1958. However, during the war years another great collector was beginning to purchase sporting art. Walter Hutchinson had long been interested in such painting. In December 1943 he purchased – through his agent, the dealer Jack Ellis – two magnificent Stubbses, *Gimcrack* and *Turf*, from Christie's and announced that they would form the nucleus of a 'National Gallery of British Sports and Pastimes'. He achieved this goal in the heart of London at Derby House, Stratford Place, where the collection looked superb in magnificent surroundings. However, the dream was short-lived for, after his untimely death, the 600 paintings were sold in three sales at Christie's in 1951–52. *Gimcrack* fetched £12,600 and at last 'it was

A study by John Dalby of a pointer at work over moorland, 1844.

recognised that, in his uncorrupted integrity, Stubbs was one of the very greatest of English masters, if not the greatest of all'. To their everlasting disgrace our public collections failed to purchase a single work from this important sale. Fortunately *Gimcrack* remains in an English private collection, but *Turf*, which fetched a mere £5,500, is now in the Mellon Collection.

Paul Mellon, whose collection surpasses any in Britain, has been the main influence in the revival of interest in sporting art after the Second World War. Although he had inherited a Marshall, bought by his father in 1935, and purchased *Pumpkin* by Stubbs when he was at Cambridge, Paul Mellon only started to collect English paintings, and especially sporting paintings, in 1959. It took an American collector to make the English look again at their sporting art heritage. The sixties were marvellous years for buying. The choice was wide, the prices reasonable and Mellon the perfect collector. Not only was he a self-

A shooting scene from 1833 by Martin Theodore Ward.

Harriers in kennels by
Thomas Henwood, 1842.

admitted 'galloping Anglophile' but, as Sir Geoffrey Agnew wrote, 'he buys
paintings because he loves them and because they give him happiness. Surely
those are the best possible reasons to collect art? His collections are very personal, and the best remembered collections are those which reveal the personality
behind them'.

Judy Egerton's superb catalogue of the collection *British Sporting and Animal
Paintings 1655–1867*, published by the Tate Gallery in 1978, is not only a worthy
record of a great collection but also the first published academic approach to
the subject.

During the 1960s a second American, Jack Dick, entered the field and his
competition with Mellon led to a rapid increase in prices. Dick, however, often
referred to as a 'great collector', was in fact a forerunner of all that is bad in
collecting. Although, with the massive funds available, he did purchase great
paintings, his collection was not at all balanced and he was little more than
a compulsive buyer of any painting by a leading name in sporting art. There
was no aesthetic or even sporting approach to his purchases and certainly no
love of painting. He was the first of the new 'investor–collectors', who do little
more than increase prices of all paintings in whatever field they select, whether
good, bad or indifferent.

The dispersal of the Dick Collection by Sotheby's in four sales between 1973
and 1976 was probably the last chance of seeing such a quantity of sporting
art on the market. The first sale, held at the height of the property boom, saw
some remarkable prices, far beyond the market value in real terms.

The Tired Hunter by Abraham Cooper, 1855.

What scope is there today for the collector interested in sporting art? The opportunity of forming a collection of Mellon proportions is simply not feasible. The cost would be prohibitive and the choice no longer available. There are few new discoveries or even neglected artists to reappraise in the period 1700 to 1850. It is, however, still possible to form a choice collection of sporting art even if restricted to the small number to furnish a house. To show what is available on the market I have chosen to illustrate this chapter with a selection of paintings and drawings that have either passed through our hands at Ackermann's or are still at the time of writing on the market. I have attempted to select a diversity of both subject matter and artists and found the end result to be encouraging in its breadth and quality. It is especially worth considering works painted in the second half of the nineteenth century. There are many paintings of merit, sometimes by quite minor artists, that have up to now been neglected.

However there are caveats of which any prospective buyer must be aware. First, condition. Naturally, over the years, paintings require cleaning and relin-

PLATE 8   Examples of James Pollard as coaching artist: *Stage Coaches at the White Horse Cellar,*
Piccadilly, 1836 (*above*) and *The Royal Mails at the Angel Inn, Islington,* 1827 (*below*).

PLATE 9   Two fishing studies by James Pollard: at Beddington Corner,
Surrey (*above*) and on the river Lea, *c* 1840 (*below*).

PLATE 10   (*above*) William
Danby shooting near
Swinton, Yorkshire, by
J. C. Ibbetson, *c* 1815.

(*left*) A shooting scene by
an enthusiastic sportsman-
artist, F. C. Turner, *c* 1835.

PLATE 11   (*above*) A portrait of Sir Robert Keith Dick with his filly Bravura, James Robinson up, by Ben Marshall, 1825. (*below*) George Mure, of Herringwell, Master of the East Suffolk hunt, with his hounds and hunt servants, by Harry Hall, *c* 1845.

ing, and regrettably, in many instances, this has not been well executed. For your own pleasure and for long term investment condition is of the utmost importance. It is therefore imperative that the collector looks closely at as many paintings as possible before buying. This should be done not only at dealers' galleries but also in the salerooms. Both are excellent sources, but both have their pitfalls. If you like what you see hanging in a gallery, make yourself known to the dealer and tell him about your interests and ask questions about his paintings. All dealers specialise and therefore are, or should be, extremely knowledgeable about the goods they may have for sale. You will discover there are many types of dealer, ranging from those who have an obvious love for their subject and are delighted to share their enthusiasm, to those who are little more than superb salesmen whose main interest is the profit margin. The second category may sell you an example of what is immediately fashionable and therefore should show a quick return on your money, but will not necessarily prove a source of long-term enjoyment.

In the salerooms you can of course buy more cheaply, for the simple reason that you are not paying the dealer's mark-up. However, it must be remembered that the salerooms do not act as principals but only as agents acting for the seller which simply means achieving the highest price possible. It is therefore

A stallion with two grey mares, painted in 1860 by Henry Barraud.

not humanly possible for their advice to a buyer to be unbiased. Secondly, the cataloguing is not necessarily as expert as it should be. This is only natural when you consider the wide range of paintings an auctioneer has to sell when compared with the specialist dealer.

Another temptation to avoid at auction is buying a big name at what seems a reasonable price. There are few bargains to be had in today's market and if the estimate in the sale catalogue, or equally the price in a dealer's gallery, is lower than you have come to expect, you should be aware that all is not well. It could be that the painting in question is not in good condition or it may simply be a bad example of the artist's work. It must be remembered that even the greatest artists have their off-days – a row with their wife or mistress, or a hangover can easily have produced an inferior work. Also the sheer quantity of work produced by such an artist as J. F. Herring Snr must perforce produce some inferior paintings.

But the biggest caveat of all is not to buy with a view of investment only. Prices of paintings have at least kept pace with inflation and sometimes achieved a great deal more, but the first and only maxim for buying any work of art is that it gives you pleasure. All other considerations are secondary.

Fashion of course affects prices as does the world financial situation, but generally sporting art is not as much affected as other schools of painting. Its very Englishness in its liking for the frank and unpretentious, for fresh observations, sound draughtsmanship and quiet humour, not to mention its subject matter, has appealed to buyers for over 300 years. Horace Walpole, for example, one of the greatest connoisseurs, chose Wootton's painting of his dog 'Patapan' to hang in his bedroom.

Perhaps the final words should be those of Gerald Reitlinger who in the third and final volume of his brilliant *Economics of Taste* wrote that 'the notion of art as an investment has created more press publicity for auction sales than has ever existed before. At the height of the sales season a record price is claimed for something or other almost every working day. One wonders whether the purpose of the writer is to show that very soon anything you buy will have become a gold mine, or whether it is to advise the Inland Revenue what to tax next. More than half these records are not records at all. Obviously it is no part of a saleroom correspondent's business to point out that the so-called record price is expressed in pounds that are worth less than a fifth of a gold sovereign. It cannot be denied that enormous profits have been made in the past two decades by those who followed fashionable trends, regardless of cost, in order to sell out a few years later, but these are not investors but speculators. The only investors are those who never meant to invest at all'.

3

THE SPORTING PRINT

JOHN SABIN

Following education at St Paul's, John Sabin fulfilled his tour of
National Service with the Royal Artillery. He then joined his father in the
family firm of of art dealers, which has long enjoyed the reputation of selling
the finest English paintings and prints. He went to Ackermann's as joint
Managing Director in 1985. Acknowledged as the leading expert
in sporting prints he has lectured widely on the subject, his
last milestone in his series of talks being the
British Sporting Art Trust's Mellon Lecture in 1986.

A line engraving by L. Truchy and C. Canot from a painting by John Wootton
in the hall at Longleat. It is from a series of scenes depicting the 2nd Viscount
Weymouth and his hounds.

The casual visitor paying his entrance fee to the National Trust's Clandon Park in Surrey may be forgiven for failing to notice the large prints hanging in the entrance hall. But in doing so he misses the opportunity of studying the set of four line-engravings of Hare Hunting – *The Going Out in the Morning, The Chace, The Hounds at Fault* and *The Death of the Hare*, which mark the beginning of the story of British sporting prints. In 1727 John Wootton paid the Frenchman Bernard Baron £50 to engrave each copper plate from his oil paintings, a vast sum at the time. Despite the time and expenditure taken on the production, the venture was evidently not a success. There was no copyright law in England at the time, and, in a matter of a few months of Wootton putting his sets on sale, inferior copies could be bought in London print shops at far cheaper prices.

It was not until 1735 that William Hogarth's Copyright Act became law and went some way to protecting the rights of the legitimate printmaker. When Wootton's magnificent paintings of Viscount Weymouth hunting, which hang in the Great Hall at Longleat, were engraved by Canot and Truchy, the prints bear, below their delightful rococo titles, the inscription 'Licensed and Published pursuant to ye VIII of George ye II'. These must be among the first engravings published once the new act came into force.

The seventeenth century had seen printed engravings of sporting pastimes, usually produced in book form, such as the Duke of Newcastle's *New System of Horsemanship*, engraved from the drawings of Abraham van Diepenbeck, in 1658, and Richard Blome's *Gentleman's Recreation*, of 1686. Wootton, however, pioneered the concept of publishing a series of engravings depicting the main stages of a hunt for the collector to frame or preserve in his folio.

Wootton, Peter Tillemans and James Seymour earned their living predominantly from commissions to paint racehorses. The horses were usually bred for staying power rather than speed, and race meetings were held on open ground where anyone could watch. The first important prints of such meetings were three line-engravings by du Bosc, T. Sympson and J. Sympson Snr, from paintings by Tillemans, of Newmarket. The pictures are *A Horse Match over the Long Course, A View of the Round-Course or Plate Course with Divers Jockeys and Horses in different Actions and Postures Going to Start for the King's Plate*, and *View of the Noblemen's and Gentlemen's Several Strings or Trains of Running Horses taking their Exercise up ye Watering-Course on the Warren Hill at Newmarket*. Their large size necessitated the use of two copper plates for each scene.

Line-engraving and mezzotint were the methods of print making in the middle of the eighteenth century. Using these techniques small racing and hunting sets, together with several series of racehorse portraits after Seymour, William Shaw, Wootton and Thomas Spencer were produced. Engravings could be bought plain or coloured in the London print shops, the most prominent of which was Robert Sayer's in Fleet Street. Prices for sets were usually a few shillings, with the buyer paying twice as much for coloured examples. The colour was gouache, sometimes known as body colour, rather crudely applied but creating a decorative effect.

William Woollett was the leading exponent of the now established group of English line-engravers of the 1760s and 1770s who had learned from the Frenchmen of the previous generation. He specialised in classical, mythological and historical subjects. In 1768 he engraved, for Thomas Bradford, *The Spanish Pointer*, after George Stubbs. In the following three years he produced for the same publisher engravings of Stubbs's four scenes of shooting in Derbyshire, the first

A sporting dinner, colour etching with aquatint, 1787, by Thomas Rowlandson. J. Harris reprinted the plate in 1798.

62

Stubbs's *Mambrino*, a stipple engraving by his son, George Townley Stubbs, for the Turf Gallery, 1794.

major shooting subjects and one of the outstanding sets to be published in the eighteenth century.

The more important early engravings were never coloured. Gouache colour was added only to the cheaper, smaller productions to widen their appeal – at a price. Even Woollett's shooting set was never coloured, despite the large numbers printed. Many prints from this period were coloured in the nineteenth century or later. The mezzotint process, ideal as it had been and would continue to be, for reproducing the effect of draperies and flesh tints in portrait painting was unsuited to the sporting scene since colour could not be effectively added to the tone. The gouache colour added to line-engravings had an attractive, but unrealistic, result.

The introduction into England from France of the aquatint process of engraving began the era of popular print production. Paul Sandby first used the technique commercially in 1775 to engrave his own topographical views. The outline of the subject was first etched onto the copper plate, then the aquatint ground laid to provide subtle variations of shade and tone. At first, little colour was added, printing often being done in brown or grey, but, as the English water-colour school developed, so did the range and quality of print colouring. At the same time major improvements in the quality of printing paper helped the establishment of the aquatint process.

Thomas Rowlandson was one of the first artists to use this process, translating his superb freedom of drawing line to the etched plate and used the aquatint ground to add depth and tone. Between 1786 and 1788 he produced a series

63

of six splendid hunting scenes in his own inimitable style and followed in 1799 with a set of four entitled *The High Mettled Racer* with ground added by J. Hassell. These subjects have great spirit but even more effective for their beautiful compositions are his scenes of the chase, near Eton and Windsor, a set of four published by Rudolph Ackermann in 1801. All these etchings with aquatint were strongly coloured in the manner of Rowlandson's early drawing style.

Many of Stubbs's racehorse pictures, such as *Mambrino*, *Gimcrack*, *Marske* and *Eclipse*, were mezzotinted by his son George Townley Stubbs, Thomas Burke, Benjamin Green and C. H. Hodges. But when, in 1794, Stubbs decided to paint a series of over 145 pictures (to illustrate *The Turf Review*) to be engraved by his son, the stipple method was used. Large and small plates were made of each subject and examples printed in both colours and black, but only 14 subjects were completed, a small version of the Godolphin Arabian being given free to subscribers. This grandiose scheme, however, failed, due perhaps to economic difficulties caused by war with France.

The last decade of the eighteenth century also saw the production of a vast number of mezzotint and stipple engravings – by John Raphael Smith, William Ward, James Ward and their followers – of domestic and country scenes, which have come to epitomise the romanticised view of the time in contemporary eyes. Morland supplied the paintings for many of these prints, including a set of four large foxhunting scenes, mezzotints by E. Bell, published in 1800–1.

Thomas Rowlandson's individual style influenced the work of his brother-in-law, Samuel Howitt. This can be clearly seen in Edward Orme's famous publication *British Field Sports*, which consisted of 20 coloured aquatints depicting foxhunting, harehunting, shooting, racing and coursing. The series is rightly considered one of the finest productions of the era. It was produced in parts of two plates each during the years 1807–8.

The pictures of J. N. Sartorius were transferred to the copper plate in line, stipple and aquatint. Notable amongst these are a set of four foxhunting in line by J. Peltro and J. Neagle, and a pair of aquatints by J. W. Edy illustrating *The Match between the Celebrated Hambletonian and Diamond*.

More than any other sporting artist Henry Alken captures the flavour of field sports in the 1820s and 1830s. Painter in oils and watercolours, etcher and aquatinter, he was master of all, and an impeccable draughtsman. His approach to his art was journalistic, reporting the activities of the famous personalities of the field, Squire Osbaldeston, Sir Harry Goodricke, Dick Christian, Hugo Meynell and John Mytton, to name a few. His output was enormous. All the important London print publishers, including S. J. Fuller, Rudolph Ackermann and Thomas McLean, used his talents. Book illustrations occupied a great deal of his time. The best known of these was *The National Sports of Great Britain*, first published by McLean in 1820, and much reprinted.

Alken executed the original drawings for this set, which were then aquatinted by J. Clark. Besides foxhunting, shooting, fishing and racing, the subjects included cock-fighting, bull-baiting, badger-baiting, beagling and otter hunting.

Handsome sets published from his originals include *The Leicestershire Covers*, aquatinted by Thomas Sutherland in 1824, and in the same year *Fox Hunting* and *Racing*, each a set of four, aquatinted by the artist himself and Sutherland. Some of the more important sets were sold in printed wrappers, although it would be rare to find any still preserved thus.

Ackermann issued Alken's *The Grand Leicestershire Steeplechase*, a set of eight, in this form in 1830. Also sold in wrappers was *The Beaufort Hunt*, aquatinted by Alken in 1833 from the originals of Walter Parry Hodges, a Dorset amateur artist. Unusually, the name of the colourist, F. Rosenberg, is printed below the dedication. A further plate, *Consequences* was added in 1834. Alken's next outstanding series of foxhunting scenes was *The Quorn Hunt*, published by Rudolph Ackermann in 1835. These eight scenes are distinguished by a strong etched line by the artist himself with the aquatint ground added by F. C. Lewis. This ground fades out almost completely in reprints. Other excellent prints after

An example from Henry Alken's *The Quorn Hunt: The pace begins to Tell!*. This is from F. C. Lewis's aquatint of the original.

Alken of the 1830s are a set of shooting, *The Moor*, *The Wood*, *The Field*, and *The Water*, engraved by the artist; and *The First Steeplechase on Record* or *The Night Riders of Nacton*, four plates engraved by J. Harris, rare in the original publication by Ackermann of 1839, but frequently seen reprinted by Ben Brooks.

The first coloured aquatints of classic winning horses are those from the paintings of J. F. Herring Snr. His paintings of St Leger winners were published by Sheardown, in Doncaster, each year from 1815, and the first ten were engraved by Thomas Sutherland. This early group was published in printed paper wrappers with a list of subscribers. In 1827 publication of the St Leger winners, together with those of the Derby, was taken over by Fuller in London, who continued until 1841. During this period the first impressions, which were subscribed, bear the Minerva Head blind stamp of the publisher. The engravers were usually Charles Hunt and R. G. Reeve and these two series represent some of the best productions of the coloured aquatint medium.

Bay Middleton, the winner of the Derby Stakes at Epsom, 1836. This aquatint engraving by C. Hunt is from the portrait by J. F. Herring Snr.

FLY FISHING.

James Pollard has always been closely associated with coaching scenes. Among his London scenes are *The Elephant and Castle on the Brighton Road* by Theodore Fielding, published by J. Watson, 1826; *West Country Mails at the Gloucester Coffee House, Piccadilly*, by C. Rosenberg, published by McLean, 1828; *The Royal Mails at the Angel Inn, Islington, on the night of His Majesty's Birth Day*, by R. G. Reeve, published by McLean; *Approach to Christmas* by G. Hunt, published by J. Moore; and *The Royal Mails Preparing to Start for the West of England* by F. Rosenberg, published by J. Watson, 1831.

Pollard's racing, hunting and fishing scenes lend themselves admirably to the aquatint process. The artist, himself a keen fisherman, painted a pair of oils, *Trolling for Pike* and *Fly Fishing*, beautifully aquatinted by George Hunt for J. Moore, and a set of four of similar scenes aquatinted by R. G. Reeve for T. Helme in 1831 and 1833. As in the coaching scenes the divergence of Pollard's style is seen in the published racing subjects. He engraved his own drawings of Doncaster, Newmarket and Ascot, meticulously reproducing tiny figures and

Fly Fishing. A coloured aquatint by George Hunt after James Pollard. Published by J. Moore, 1831

67

horses, in a joint publication with his father, Robert, in 1818. These contrast with his mature style of the late 1830s exemplified in the set of six *Epsom* scenes, aquatinted by Charles Hunt for Ackermann in 1836, a set of four: *British Horse Racing, Goodwood, Epsom, Ascot* and *Doncaster*, engraved by R. G. Reeve, published by McLean in the same year, and a further set of four *Doncaster Races, The St Leger of 1836*, aquatinted by J. Harris for Ackermann in 1837.

Considering their importance in British sporting art, Ben Marshall and John Ferneley Snr painted little for the print makers. Certainly, in Ferneley's case, he was kept busy enough at Melton without the need to work for London publishers. A few of Ben Marshall's paintings of the characters of the hunting field were considered of enough public interest to merit publication. *The Earl of Darlington and his Fox Hounds*, engraved in a mixture of line and stipple by J. Dean, was also printed in colour and published in 1805 by the artist himself.

The careers of Dean Wolstenholme Snr and Jnr cover a long period in the commercial use of the aquatint engraving technique and admirably illustrate its development from the rather crude productions of the early 1800s to the delicate grains of the 1830s. Apart from the occasional coursing and shooting subjects, they concentrate almost entirely on hunting scenes in Essex, Hertfordshire and Surrey. Wolstenholme Snr's work lent itself particularly well to the aquatint process and those engraved by his son have a special appeal.

Although the aquatint process dominated print production in the first half of the nineteenth century, other techniques were not entirely ignored. Charles Turner was an excellent practitioner of mezzotint, usually working the plate with other engraving tools to enhance the range of effects. These were occasionally colour printed, such as *Preparing to Start* and *Coming In*, a fine pair of racing scenes after J. L. Agasse, published 1802–3; *Dash* (a setter), also after Agasse, published by Ackermann, and *Mr Saml Chifney*, a splendid portrait of the famous jockey probably based on the engraver's own sketch and published by him in 1807.

The popular sporting aquatint developed over several decades from 1790 when Charles Loraine Smith illustrated the exploits of Dick Knight in the *Pytchley Hunt*, a set of eight engraved by Francis Jukes. Despite the advent of cheaper production methods such as lithography and the steel plate, the aquatint was in common use up to the 1880s. One of the largest foxhunting sets was engraved by W. Summers after John Sturges in 1878. The invention of the steel plate, however, fundamentally changed the print selling scene. These plates had a much longer life than copper, and hundreds of impressions could be taken. It was used for example, to reproduce the paintings of Sir Francis Grant. *The Melton Breakfast* (1838), *The Meet at Melton* (1841) and *Sir Richard Sutton and the Quorn Hounds*, are among his best known work.

In the heyday of the popular sporting print, engravers must have been kept extraordinarily busy, considering they were not working solely on sporting subjects. In particular, Rudolph Ackermann was publishing books with aquatinted colour plate on the arts, costume, architecture, topography and travel on a large

THE RENDEZVOUS.

Aquatint by R. G. Reeve
after F. C. Turner:
*Hawking: The
Rendezvous, c1837.*

scale, and the total output of the most skilled of these craftsmen was enormous, but they appear to have received little recognition at the time. James Ward, tired of mezzotinting for his brother William, went on to become one of our great romantic painters. Edward Duncan and Charles Bentley had success as watercolourists, and both William Ward and Charles Turner succeeded as publishers. Charles Lane shows in his exhaustive study of the aquatinters that many struggled to make a reasonable living, despite long and hardworking careers.

Unfortunately, the number of sporting prints on public view in Britain is limited. The group in the British Museum covers a wide variety of subject and an excellent selection was exhibited in the print room in 1983. The well-illustrated catalogue of that exhibition is worth owning for its introduction and comments on the exhibits.

To extend his knowledge the enthusiast needs to visit the auction houses for the few print sales which now take place in the calendar year, and call on the specialist dealers where prints of sports and pastimes can be studied.

Reprints

Reprints fall into two groups. The print sellers either sold on their engraved plates to other businesses, who changed the publication line accordingly, or, as happened frequently in the early nineteenth century, the plate would be reprinted without alteration to the imprint

A change of publication line can be noted and recorded and this information is available to the collector and enthusiast, but, when reprints were taken from unaltered plates, the problem of determining the true date and authenticity becomes more complex. The type of paper and quality of engraving become the two vital factors; in the late 1830s Whatman-type papers were gradually replaced by heavier thicker papers, used, for example, by Fores for their well-known *Coaching Recollections* and *Coaching Incidents*, after C. Henderson, and the larger Herring and Alken racing and hunting scenes of the 1840s and later.

Since reprints were, in some cases, made as little as five years after the original publication, the plates had little wear, and it is obviously difficult to distinguish differences, particularly when a print is viewed under glass. Good examples are the Fuller publications of Herring classic winners, which were reprinted extensively on thick paper. Copper plates wore quickly, but only very occasionally do we know the number of impressions printed, and if demand was small the quality of reprinting can be remarkably good. Rapid wear, in the aquatint process particularly, caused the ground to disappear leaving a strong etched line. The quality of colouring deteriorated in the latter half of the nineteenth century, often becoming crude and heavy to cover up the deficiencies of the worn plate.

Although a certain amount of knowledge of reprints can be gleaned from books on old sporting prints, there is no substitute for the experience of studying and handling the prints themselves so as to appreciate the types of paper and the gradual changes in paper production. Such study will also give an understanding of the results of the various engraving techniques and the changes brought about by wear and the reworking of copper.

Engraving Techniques
Etching
The copper plate is covered with a layer of wax, then the design is drawn, exposing the copper. Next, the plate is dipped in a bath of acid which bites into the copper. The plate is then wiped clean of wax with turpentine, leaving it ready for use.

Pigeon Shooting: Members of the Red House Club shooting for the Gold Cup (1828). Aquatint by R. G. Reeve after Henry Alken.

Line-engraving

The copper is cut into by means of the graver or burin. The raised copper, known as burr, is removed by means of the scraper to leave clear-cut lines, which can be made as deep as required.

Mezzotint

The mezzotint is a tone process. The surface of the copper plate is roughed up by a tool called a rocker which has a curved edge with cutting teeth. This is worked over the surface to raise a burr. The engraver then scrapes away the burr, working from dark to light. A mezzotint is often described as 'scraped'. The lighter the area required the more copper has to be removed.

The colour-printed mezzotint was obtained by applying the colour direct to the single plate by means of a 'dolly', a piece of rag attached to the end of a stick. The plate had to be freshly coloured for each impression.

Stipple

The plate is prepared as for etching. As the name implies the design is produced by dots made through the wax. However, the dotting and design is continued directly on the plate by the use of other engraving tools and roulettes.

The stipple engraving in colour was obtained by applying colour with a 'dolly' as in colour mezzotint engraving. The plate is wiped clean and the colours left in the hollows and the subsequent print producing separate dots of colour. The chief exponents of the stipple method were Francesco Bartolozzi and his followers.

71

Another of J. Moore's publications: colour aquatinted by Charles Hunt after a painting by J. F. Herring Snr, it depicts the dead heat between Charles XII and Euclid for the Doncaster Great St Leger in 1839.

Aquatint

This method produces transparent tone effects, the tone being obtained by biting with acid (*aqua fortis*). A porous ground is laid on the plate to control the action of the acid. Resin is dissolved in alcohol and on evaporation the resin is left on the plate in tiny grains. The acid is allowed to bite into the exposed copper for as long as is required. Areas that are not to be bitten are protected by varnish. The outline design of sporting prints was usually etched on the plate before the aquatint process was begun.

Soft-ground Etching

This is used to reproduce accurately the effect of pencil drawing. The plate is covered with wax mixed with tallow so that it remains soft. The design is then drawn with pencil on thin paper laid on the ground. When the paper is removed the tallow attaches to the paper where pressed by the pencil. The exposed copper is bitten with acid and this gives an excellent print of the pencil grain.

Lithography

The design is drawn on a slab of limestone using greasy chalk, then the stone is washed with acid. The greased area retains the printing ink from a roller and the design is transferred to paper. Printing requires only slight pressure and no plate mark results.

72

4

A DEALER'S VIEWPOINT, II
THE TWENTIETH CENTURY

CLAUDE BERRY

Educated at Wellington and Sandhurst and commissioned into the
16th/5th Lancers, Claude Berry served in Aden, Germany and Malaya. On leaving
the Army, he worked on a farm in Gloucestershire before studying at the
Royal Agricultural College, Cirencester. He then farmed for 16 years in
Roxburghshire, during which time he qualified as a chartered surveyor. Also a
breeder, trainer and rider of racehorses, he bred a winner of the
Italian Derby and of the French St Leger.
In 1978 he joined the staff of the Tryon Gallery, of which he has been a
director since 1980. He is the art correspondent of *The European Racehorse*,
and is on the executive committee of the British Sporting Art Trust.

The Sanctuary by Raoul Millais, 1977. The grandson of the pre-Raphaelite
co-founder and President of the Royal Academy, Raoul Millais has been a
lifelong stalking man, foxhunter and fisherman.

For the sporting art collector of limited means the twentieth century is undoubtedly the most rewarding period. Good examples of the work of the best earlier sporting painters are now beyond the reach of all but a small minority of collectors. It is, however, possible to buy good pictures by the leading artists of this century for less than £10,000 and, by concentrating on living artists, very good sporting pictures can still be bought for under £1,000.

Contemporary artists, particularly the less successful ones, frequently complain that nobody wishes to buy their pictures until they are dead. There is a measure of truth in this complaint and, where it applies, the astute collector may benefit from the reluctance of certain established collectors to buy the work of living artists. Certainly the last decade has seen some dramatic examples of how the prices of certain artists' work have increased spectacularly very shortly after the death of the artist in question. John Skeaping died in 1980 and the racing pictures he painted in the late 1970s are now worth at least ten times what they cost then. Two further examples of this tendency are the bird painters Charles Frederick Tunnicliffe (d. 1979) and John Cyril Harrison (d. 1985).

Collecting pictures is an intensely personal pastime. 'One man's meat is another man's poison'. The important thing is to buy what you like. It is pointless to buy a picture in which some small detail irritates you. Although you may feel that you will grow to like the picture as time goes on, you will be wrong. The passage of time is almost certain to increase rather than decrease your irritation.

From time to time I am approached by people whose first question is likely to be 'Is this a good investment?' I regard this as a poor opening gambit because, as the conversation unfolds, this type of buyer invariably turns out to have little or no interest in the picture itself or in the artist concerned. His sole aim is to achieve capital appreciation. My usual advice to such an enquirer is that he should consult a stockbroker rather than an art dealer.

I cannot overemphasise how important it is for the collector to buy something which he likes and which will give him pleasure for many years. Trust in your own judgement and try not to be swayed by that fickle mistress 'fashion'. The point of a collection is to give pleasure to the owner, not to astonish others.

It would be a dull world if we all liked the same things. Thus each gallery will specialize in the work of a certain number of artists to the exclusion of others. Try to visit as many galleries as possible. It is only in this way that you will be able to make your own judgements. Never hesitate to question the gallery staff about an artist whose work attracts you. The staff are employed to answer your questions. More than 90 per cent of the people who come to our gallery

A 'thirties painting by
G. D. Armour: *The Last
Fence*.

leave without buying anything and no visitor should feel at all guilty at leaving
empty-handed. Although it is unusual to leave a supermarket without making
a purchase, it is the norm where art galleries are concerned.

Having emphasised how no two people will admire the work of exactly the
same artists, I propose now to write about some of those twentieth century artists
whose work I particularly enjoy. This list will obviously not be comprehensive
and it may well be that some of your favourites are omitted. This is inevitable
in so short a review of the century and it is important that the collector should
not rely too heavily on the opinions of others.

The work of the American photographer Eadweard Muybridge in the last
two decades of the nineteenth century had a more dramatic effect on artists than

76

the work of any individual before or since. His series of still plates of a horse cantering, a horse jumping and a man running opened the eyes of artists to what actually happened to a body in movement. Many artists paid no attention to Muybridge's work and continued to paint the galloping horse in the *ventre à terre* position. I regard those artists as being basically Victorian painters, even though some of them did not die until well into this century.

The best sporting artists are, almost without exception, those who take part in the sports which they depict. As Sir Alfred Munnings wrote, 'He who paints people and horses must ride himself'. It is only by participating that the artist can capture the feel of the sport and can avoid those elementary mistakes at once apparent to the sportsman, but which are hidden from the uninitiated.

The history of British sporting art has been mainly the history of the horse, because painters have concentrated on hunting, racing and polo to a much greater extent than on those sports in which the horse has no part to play. The only first flight artist of this century who has painted every country sport convincingly is Lionel Edwards, but more of him later. I propose to concentrate first on those painters whose main subject was the horse and it may be helpful if I deal with them in roughly chronological order.

George Denholm Armour (1864–1949) is a particular favourite of mine: he was a thorough sportsman and his work shows a sense of humour by no means

Coursing: another painting by G. D. Armour, *c*1920.

universal amongst artists. Much of his youth was spent in Scotland: he was born in Lanarkshire, went to school in Fife and attended art school in Edinburgh. As a young man he went to Tangier with fellow artist and Scot, Robert Alexander, and while there became a close friend of Joseph Crawhall whose work he greatly admired. For a period Crawhall was first whip to the Tangier hounds while Armour acted as second whip. On his return to England he took a studio in the Fulham Road and contributed to many magazines. His sporting cartoons were a feature of *Punch* for the first thirty years of this century. He was a good horseman and rough rider and dealt successfully in horses bought at Tattersalls. This form of income helped to pay for his hunting, first with the Beaufort and, after the First World War, with the South Berks and Sparkford Vale Harriers.

During the war he served with the Army Remount Service and ended up as Director of Remounts in Macedonia. He was awarded the OBE for his military services. A truly versatile sportsman and limner, he was equally happy illustrating shooting, fishing, stalking, racing or polo but his main love was always hunting. Armour died at the age of eighty-five in 1949. I have ceased to be amazed at the longevity of artists and can only conclude that their lives must be free of the stresses which drive many of their non-creative contemporaries into early graves.

Arthur Wardle was an exact contemporary of Armour and yet he is more

Pointers by Arthur Wardle, *c*1935.

78

Victorian in his approach. He was at his best when painting dogs although he did produce some major hunting canvases. Curiously enough these are usually spoiled by the wooden appearance of his hounds whose heads would send any serious hound breeder in search of the humane killer.

The brothers George and Gilbert Wright painted many attractive hunting pictures. George (1860–1942) was 20 years older than Gilbert but the pair often worked together until Gilbert became established. They painted a large number of coaching pictures, the figures frequently being in period costume, and a few racing pictures. George was the better artist of the two although the prices of both have increased dramatically in recent years.

The work of Lynwood Palmer (1868–1939) seldom comes onto the market because the majority of his paintings were commissions and have remained in the families for whom they were painted. He was a man of determined character who ran away to Canada at the age of 17 to avoid being forced into the law or the diplomatic service. He returned to England in 1899 and was soon busily engaged on commission work. He painted *Minoru* for King Edward VII and *Scuttle* for King George V, but his masterpiece is probably *The 6th Duke of Portland's Horses at Welbeck Abbey*. Many of his paintings, including this fine picture, were very large.

Whereas many of the leading horse painters of today are women, good female painters were formerly something of a rarity. An exception to this rule was Lucy Kemp-Welch (1869–1958). Displaying a precocious talent, she sold her first drawing when only 16 and had her first picture accepted by the Royal Academy at the age of 26. She was not yet 30 when her *Colt Hunting in the New Forest* was bought by the Tate Gallery, a rare honour for a woman artist at that time. She was elected president of the Society of Animal Painters, among whose members were Alfred Munnings and Lionel Edwards. She worked in oils, watercolour and pastel and, in addition to her sporting studies, painted many First World War pictures and scenes of circus life. Her final Royal Academy exhibit was accepted when she was 80 years old and she became a recluse in her declining years.

An artist whose work is, in my view, insufficiently appreciated is Alfred Grenfell Haigh (1870–1963), yet another who exceeded by a considerable margin his threescore years and ten. He was educated at Rossall, studied in Paris and went to live at Newmarket at the turn of the century. He soon attracted the notice of the racing fraternity and most of his work consisted of racehorse and hunting commissions. For this reason, as with Lynwood Palmer, his work seldom comes onto the market. Although he never attempted to capture any extravagant movement in his subjects, his pictures are invariably interesting, attractive and of good quality. They are well worth the attention of any serious collector.

Cecil Aldin (1870–1935) has recently acquired a large number of devotees but I have to confess that I am not among them. His work commands prices which I find surprising. As a portrayer of dogs he is superb and, like Armour, he had an excellent sense of humour which is particularly well shown in his illustrations

(above) A 1911 portrait by
Alfred Haigh: The Duke of
Beaufort's huntsman, Will
Dale, and hounds. (right)
Alfred Haigh at work,
painting Bahram, c1936.

80

for Surtees's *Handley Cross*. However his major series of hunting countries, the prints of which are well known, are stiff and stilted and the anatomy of his horses compares unfavourably with those of Munnings, Edwards or Holiday. Despite this he is a major figure in twentieth century sporting art and the fact that I consider him to be overrated at present only goes to show, as I have mentioned before, that 'one man's meat . . . . .'

The years 1877–79 saw the birth of four of the most important equestrian artists of the century – Stewart, Munnings, Edwards and Holiday.

Frank Algernon Stewart (1877–1945) has always suffered from being in the shadow of Lionel Edwards but he was a very competent watercolourist who thoroughly understood hunting. After service as a war artist in South Africa he was invalided home and then went to study in Paris. On his return to England he hunted with many packs and produced excellent watercolours. Some of his pictures were reproduced as limited edition prints, others in book form. His major pictures were usually long and narrow in shape which enabled him to give a good impression of the country over which hounds were hunting and, as with Aldin, many of the figures represented were leading members of the hunt. Although lacking the flair and freedom of Edwards his work is much more true to life than that of Aldin. In my view his major watercolours deserve to fetch considerably higher prices than they do and I feel that they are certain to rise in the wake of the current increase in the price of Edwards's and Holiday's work.

Having mentioned Stewart's hunting prints I would like to digress for a moment to sound a word of warning. Twentieth-century hunting prints are a feature of many country houses and homes of nostalgic city dwellers. Edwards and Munnings prints are very liable to fade and the risk increases with the passage of time. Indeed more than half the Edwards prints seen nowadays are faded. The process is irreversible and one of the golden rules for collectors is never to buy a faded print. It goes without saying that the fading process will be accelerated if the print is hung in sunlight or indeed in any bright light. While the colours of Edwards and Munnings prints are fugitive, the Stewart and Aldin prints were produced by a superior process; they are a better bet for long-term survival and indeed it is rare to find a faded Stewart or Aldin print.

It is difficult to find anything new to say about Sir Alfred Munnings (1878–1959). He is, in my opinion, the greatest sporting painter of our age and his boldness in the use of colour is breathtaking. While all who met Edwards were at once charmed by his modesty, this virtue was not the longest suit in Munnings's hand. The dramatic upsurge in the value of his work which has taken place in the last decade has placed his major pictures beyond the reach of all but the most affluent collectors. His racing pictures, in particular, have soared to heights which many find hard to justify. Unfortunately the market is now being flooded by sketches which are both unfinished and of moderate quality and which the artist, were he alive, would certainly not wish to see exhibited to the public. Collectors keen to 'have a Munnings' would do well to resist the temptation to buy one of those.

The Munnings pictures which give me the most pleasure are his gypsy scenes. One of the reasons why his pictures have the feeling of authenticity is that he worked from life and used both human and equine models whenever possible. I wish that more of the budding young artists of today would realise the importance of doing this. While almost any Munnings painting containing a horse has become prohibitively expensive, it is still possible to buy some of his landscapes for less than 'a king's ransom'.

Although Munnings is the greatest sporting painter of the century, Lionel Edwards (1878–1966) is, I suggest, the greatest hunting artist. While Munnings's best work was in oils, Edwards was more at home in gouache or watercolour. Edwards's pictures were too little appreciated after his death until the superb exhibition of his work mounted by the British Sporting Art Trust in 1986, when people finally realised what an outstanding artist he was. Since then his prices have rocketed, as they should have done several years ago. Edwards was a quick worker and his output was prodigious. He wrote and illustrated several books and, in addition, illustrated many by other authors. These books are prized by their owners and I always feel that a very worthwhile target for any collector would be to acquire a copy of every book illustrated by Edwards.

Edwards grew up in North Wales and studied under that great teacher and good painter Frank Calderon. During the First World War he joined the Army Remount Service, as did Aldin, Armour and Munnings, and spent most of the war near Romsey in Hampshire. In 1921 he and his wife Ethel settled down at Buckholt in the Hursley hunt country and this was to remain their home for the rest of their lives. From that base he travelled extensively to paint, not only the hunting pictures for which he is best known but also racing, coursing, stalking, shooting and fishing pictures. He, more than any other, is the complete sporting artist of the twentieth century.

An artist whom Edwards particularly admired was Gilbert Holiday (1879–1937). In their youth they once shared a studio, each finding the other extremely untidy. Holiday served with the Royal Field Artillery on the Western Front and many of his best pictures were of military scenes and gun teams. He was probably the first artist to profit from Muybridge's revelations and Edwards regarded him as the first successful portrayer of the horse in movement. His technique was to blur the outline of the swiftly moving parts of the horse's body and to lose the feet of the horse in dust, mud or grass. This technique was later used with great success by John Skeaping. Holiday did not enjoy as long a life as we have come to expect of most artists and his work is therefore less easy to find. He died at the age of 58, having spent his last years in a wheelchair as a result of a fall sustained while out with the Woolwich Drag. His pictures are of comparable quality to those of Lionel Edwards although his range of subject is hardly as wide. He seldom produced a bad picture.

Mention should be made of Charles Johnson Payne (1884–1967), better known as 'Snaffles'. An intensely patriotic man, he served at different times in the army, the Royal Naval Air Service and the RNVR, and he drew on his experiences

A Lionel Edwards scene on Newmarket Heath: *Early Morning*, 1926.

with all three services to produce the prints for which he is so well known. His hunting and racing prints are the most popular (a print of *An Irish Point-to-Point* will cost anything from £3,000 to £4,000) but the perennial popularity of his work owes more to his flair for capturing the emotional and nostalgic feeling for his subjects than to the artistic merit of his work.

Of those equestrian artists who were born and died during this century, four deserve our particular attention. The first of these is John Skeaping (1901–1980). Showing a precocious talent, he studied at the Goldsmiths' College, the Central School of Art and the Royal Academy Schools, winning the Gold Medal and a travelling scholarship at the last named. He served in the SAS during the war and later travelled extensively, spending a period with the Indians in Mexico. A bold horseman – he rode in races as a young man – he was also, with his second wife, a breeder and trainer of greyhounds and he is one of the few artists who has drawn convincing coursing pictures. He spent the last twenty years of his life in the Camargue.

John Skeaping is best known for his sculpture but his output of drawings was also prolific. His great talent was to convey movement and he found pastel and gouache more effective media for this purpose than oils. His best racing pictures capture the Thoroughbred in action with a skill only attained by some-one who understands his subject completely and these pictures are, in my view, still undervalued. Less sought after are his drawings of bullfighting and Arab horsemen but they are equally skilful and also rely for their effect on economy of line. The joy of Skeaping's work is that he leaves something to the imagination.

An artist whose work is not widely known but who is well worth collecting is Tom Carr (1912–1977). Born into a mining community in Co. Durham, Carr studied at King's College, Newcastle-upon-Tyne, and spent the latter part of his life a few miles north of the border in Roxburghshire. A friendly man with a dry sense of humour, his early path through life was not an easy one; I well remember him telling me, with a twinkle in his eye, how he had been forced to steal materials in his student days. Many of his hunting, racing and point-to-point pictures were commissioned and consequently seldom appear on the market. As with Skeaping, his watercolours were more successful than his oils.

As the only pupil of Lionel Edwards, Peter Biegel (1913–1987) was uniquely placed to carry on the tradition of his great mentor. His very best work is excellent and bears comparison with that of Edwards. He executed many commissions of well-known horses and his racing and hunting action pictures can be first-class. He was particularly effective when combining the use of pencil and watercolour.

Leesa Sandys-Lumsdaine (1936–1985) also spent the last years of her life

Peter Biegel: *The first Fence, Mackeson Gold Cup – 1965, Cheltenham.*

84

Another racing painting by Biegel: *They clotted my crimson!*, c1965.

among the Border hills. Like Snaffles, she is better known for her prints than for her originals. Her sense of fun pervaded her work and she invariably chose good titles for her pictures. A little drawing of a guinea pig contemplating a small vegetable was entitled '*I do like a good pea*'. Her masterpiece, reproduced as a print, was *Echoes of the Past* which won the *Horse and Hound* Centenary Art Competition and among her most popular prints were *Saturday Night and Sunday Morning* and *Absolute Heaven and Absolute Hell*.

Among those sporting artists still living the doyen is Raoul Millais (b. 1901), grandson of Sir John Everett Millais, one of the founders of the Pre-Raphaelite Brotherhood. Another pupil of Frank Calderon, he was also a contemporary of Skeaping at the Royal Academy Schools. During his long life he has painted a variety of subjects and his work possesses an elegance typical of the artist himself. Among the racing commissions he has painted have been *Big Game* and *Sun Chariot* for King George VI. A keen stalker, his stalking oils have a wide appeal and his bullfighting drawings date from the time when he and his wife spent part of every year in Spain.

Michael Lyne (b. 1912) has a considerable following both at home and in the United States. Hunting has always been his main theme but he has also produced good racing and coursing pictures. The quality of his output varies enormously but his best work is very good.

Four artists born between the wars have a considerable following. Lionel Hamilton-Renwick (b. 1919), a breeder of Shetland ponies, is best known for his racehorse commissions. John King (b. 1929), an experienced and much-travelled foxhunter, is a prolific hunting artist whose work has appeared in many books and magazines. He also paints racing and polo pictures – some of his polo sketches are particularly fluent – and has recently turned his attentions to sculpture. Peter Howell (b. 1932) uses the experience gained while working in racing stables to produce pictures in which the influence of the French Impressionists is at once evident. Much of his work is now in the United States. The same remark applies to Neil Cawthorne (b. 1936) who concentrates mainly on the hunting field and who has been much in demand for commissioned work.

Echoes of the Past by Leesa Sandys-Lumsdaine, 1984.

86

A feature, mentioned before, of the younger generation of equestrian artists is that many of the most successful are women. The outstanding exception to this rule is the Irishman Peter Curling (b. 1955). Having studied in Florence under Signorina Simi, he spent a short time with John Skeaping whose influence can be seen in his work. A bold user of colour, Curling excels in capturing the atmosphere and movement of the racecourse and of early mornings on the gallops. He hunts with the Tipperary and among his most recent work have been some excellent hunting pictures. He is a very competent landscape painter, as befits an admirer of Munnings.

Susan Crawford (b. 1941) stands supreme among women artists. The daughter of a trainer, she also studied under Signorina Simi and is the leading contemporary exponent of the traditional British school of equestrian art. She receives more commissions than she can cope with, and it is a cause of sadness to her countless admirers than her duties as the wife of a successful army officer result in her artistic output being at present so small. Her skill as a portrait painter has caused

Another Sandys-Lumsdaine study: *Winter Woolies*, 1976.

Two of Susan Crawford's racehorse studies: *Dancing Brave*, 1987 (above) and
Ela Mana Mou (W. Carson up), 1982.

PLATE 12   (*above*) *The Whip* by Sir Alfred Munnings, *c* 1933.
(*below*) *Immortals of the Turf* by Leesa Sandys-Lumsdaine, 1972.

PLATE 13 (*above*) *Sprint Finish* by Peter Curling, 1986.

(*right*) *Leytown Races*
by Constance Holford
Thompson, 1986.

PLATE 14   Falconry studies: *Goshawk on a Bow Perch* by
Mary-Clare Critchley-Salmonson, 1985, and (*left*)
Lanneret by Hendrik Slijper, 1981.

PLATE 15 *Woodcock and Pointer* by Rodger McPhail, 1986. 'With young artists of his calibre at work we can be sure that the best traditions of British Sporting Art will be carried forward into the twenty-first century'.

her to be chosen to paint many well-known figures as well as famous horses and she is equally competent in portraying all types of livestock.

Other women whose pictures are in demand include Ruth Gibbons (b. 1945), whose work depicts all types of equestrian sport, Susie Whitcombe (b. 1957), who has exhibited not only in Britain but also in Hong Kong and Japan and Clare Eva Burton who concentrates mainly on the racing scene.

While British sporting art has always been centred round the horse, I now propose to deal briefly with those field sports in which the horse has no part to play and to mention those artists whose work covers these sports.

Twentieth century shooting pictures are surprisingly rare, although the number of bird pictures is infinite. Archibald Thorburn (1860–1935) was no lover of field sports but his pictures of game birds are superb. His contemporary George Lodge (1860–1954) painted some good shooting pictures although his game birds are less good than Thorburn's. Two artists who died during the

Archibald Thorburn's portrait of Blackcock: *The Glen among the Moors*, 1911.

First World War, Frank Southgate (1872–1916) and Otto Murray Dixon (1882–1917) produced good work during their short lives, and Southgate, who was influenced by the Impressionists, is one whose pictures I particularly admire. John Cyril Harrison (1898–1985) excelled at depicting game birds in flight. There was a reluctance on the part of all these artists to show the guns in any game bird picture. (This is a peculiarly British trait; American collectors, by contrast, prefer to see guns clearly defined and, if possible, some dead birds as witness to their prowess.)

George Lodge, a keen falconer himself, was at his best when portraying birds of prey and he is one of the few artists who have produced convincing falconry pictures. The demand for these has increased recently as Arab interest has spread and one of those who has specialised in this subject is Mary-Clare Critchley-Salmonson who first came to prominence when she illustrated *Falconry in Arabia*.

In earlier centuries there has been an excellent tradition of fishing pictures in British sporting art and this tradition was carried on by Norman Wilkinson (1878–1971), the marine painter who invented the camouflage system of dazzle painting first used in the 1914–1918 war. Although I have concentrated throughout on British artists, mention should here be made of the fine American painter Ogden Pleissner (1905–1983) who painted some excellent pictures following his

Early in the Season by H. Frank Wallace, *c*1925.

Voices of the Forest, 1912. A Highland study by Archibald Thorburn, one of the great animal artists of the early twentieth century.

fishing trips to Scotland and whose prints are much in demand. Among those painting Britain's fishing rivers today William Garfit and Tim Havers have built up enthusiastic followings.

Stalking has always attracted artists, partly no doubt because the red deer is found in such a spectacular environment. Vincent Balfour-Browne (1880–1963) spent most of his life on the hill in south-west Scotland, and his watercolours, usually given narrative titles, show the sport from the stalker's viewpoint. While his deer are first-class, his game birds are less good. Frank Wallace (1881–1962) was another whose experience on the hill was reflected in his work. He also painted some good fishing pictures. Wallace collaborated with his close friend Edwards on *Hunting and Stalking the Deer*, the former writing and illustrating the Scottish section of the book while the latter dealt with the red deer on Exmoor. Millais's stalking pictures have already been mentioned while Brian Rawling's work has increased in popularity in recent years.

All the sports discussed above have been admirably illustrated by Lionel Edwards but versatility such as his is a rare gift. Few artists have such specialized knowledge and experience of all sports and without such experience their work lacks the feel of authenticity. Of those alive today the outstanding examples of this versatility are the Dutchman Rien Poortvliet and Rodger McPhail. Poortvliet's work is virtually unobtainable because he seldom parts with an original, although his enormously popular books can be bought and these demonstrate the range of his talent. McPhail, however, holds frequent exhibitions and his pictures are by no means expensive. Of the books he has illustrated the one which best exemplifies his versatility is *Open Season*. With young artists of his calibre at work we can be confident that the best traditions of British sporting art will be carried forward into the twenty-first century.

Stalker Returning Home by
Rodger McPhail, 1986.

5

THE SCULPTORS

EDWARD HORSWELL

Edward Horswell grew up in Berkshire in the ambience of his parents' extensive bird
garden and substantial collection of animal sculpture, a subject
on which his mother wrote a definitive reference book,
The Bronze Sculptures of the Animaliers. On leaving Eton, he joined his
father's engineering firm but, a little later, he settled into the
Sladmore Gallery, off Berkeley Square, the animal sculpture showrooms started
by his mother in 1969. He now runs the gallery in tandem with his partner,
Julia Hazandras. Much of his time is spent travelling – buying animal and
sporting sculpture, and researching the subject for a forthcoming book.
The name Horswell is also synonymous with the Sladmore polo team, of which
Edward, alongside his brother John, has been a member for many years. He took
up the game in his Pony Club days. In 1987 the team reached the finals of
all three national medium-goal tournaments, of which they won two.

Tiger Hunt by A. L. Barye, 1836.

From the beginning of time man has decorated his dwelling with paintings of the hunt and no doubt soon afterwards this desire to record what was an essential part of his life (in contrast to what was later to become a pleasurable pursuit) also manifested itself into the sculptural form.

From the Greek and Roman civilizations, through medieval times, right up until the beginning of the nineteenth century there had always been a strong and ever-present tradition of sporting and animal sculpture. This tradition tended to manifest itself in large bronze sculpture, usually commissioned by a wealthy patron and often including his own portrait. The height of the Industrial Revolution, and the large commercial bronze foundries that it spawned, was some years away, and consequently any bronze sculpture was extremely expensive to produce, making it a medium for only the most important commissions or occasions. That is not to say that sculpture had been neglected, although it was always considered an inferior art form, but the nineteenth century was to see it rise to a highly regarded school in its own right.

The various schools in Paris had for several generations, leading up to the first quarter of the nineteenth century, been indoctrinated with an academic approach to art, focused on the classical maxim of an adulation of the human body. The growing trend towards romanticism forced a break with this stifling academism and its human preoccupations, producing a new school of art the emphasis of which was, almost in defiance, to be based on the animal. The artist's imagination was stimulated by a general return to nature and an increased interest in the more unusual and exotic species, resulting in a large amount of sculpture being produced from the 1830s onward with the animal as its dominant theme.

The Industrial Revolution, with its more efficient techniques, enabled bronzes to be produced for the first time at a reasonable cost, and to put them within reach of the new broadening middle class. As this section of society became more affluent, with more time for hunting, racing and other sporting activities, naturally the demand for sporting art increased dramatically. Thus began the golden age of sporting sculpture, a period of 60 years that was to see more produced than at any other time before or since.

The leading figure in the coterie of sculptors, known collectively as *Les Animaliers*, was Antoine Louis Barye (1795–1875) whose 1831 salon exhibit of a Tiger and Gavial, while not exactly sporting in subject, was to help pave the way for all that was to follow. It was Barye's strong personality and unquestionable talent that was to inspire his brother-artists and create an appreciative public. His formative years were spent goldsmithing, first in his father's atelier and then with Napoleon Bonaparte's renowned goldsmith, Biennais. After studying briefly with Bosio and then Gros, Barye proceeded to spend much of his time drawing and dissecting animals, much as Stubbs did.

Although a great deal of his work is purely animal, he did create many sporting pieces, the most important being the group of nine sculptures for an elaborate table decoration commissioned by the Duke d'Orleans, in 1834. The five main sculptures depicted the hunts of the bull, lion, bear, elk and tiger, and although originally conceived in silver, in 1837 they were eventually cast in bronze; they are now in the Walters Art Gallery, Baltimore, USA, which houses the largest collection of Barye's work to be seen today.

In addition to these, Barye produced a number of smaller pieces with a sporting theme. He composed many sculptures of dogs flushing game – pointers, setters, spaniels, basset hounds and greyhounds – as well as stags, bears and horses, including one being attacked by a lion, (perhaps in some way inspired by Stubbs). From 1840 onwards, he cast these in large numbers for sale to the new middle class of Paris, who purchased them eagerly. Some were cast and finished under his own supervision, often bearing a Barye stamp and number in addition to his signature, and are generally acknowledged by experts today to be the best examples of his work. They are certainly more sought after by collectors than the profusion of more mediocre castings produced by the independent foundries from 1845 onwards.

Christopher Fratin (1800–1864), born in Metz, was the son of a taxidermist and originally studied under Pioche. Later he was accepted as a pupil by the celebrated painter Gericault and moved to Paris. Like Barye, Fratin was strongly influenced by the romantic movement at the time, but his work, being more ragged in texture, has none of the complete freedom of line that was Barye's *tour de force*, and is reminiscent of the impasto technique of his master, Gericault.

Another important sculptor from the school of *Les Animaliers* was Pierre Jules Mêne (1810–1879), who, despite working in a style that is in direct contrast to Barye – and never as renowned in his own lifetime – has emerged today as the sculptor most associated with, and typical of, the sporting models produced during the nineteenth century.

Although one or two of his earlier works show the influence of romanticism, Mêne was essentially a realist, whose overriding aim was to show his subjects as true to life as possible, this realism blending more and more with naturalism throughout his life. Barye's animal subjects are usually of a type and instantly recognisable (as a 'Barye Lion' etc.) but Mêne's subjects are almost always individual portraits, this or that dog or horse, and in many cases we know their particular names. *The Accolade* was originally entitled *Tachiani and Nejibe, Arab Horses*, and became one of Mêne's finest and most successful sculptures, being edited – in four different sizes – in considerable numbers.

One of the largest and most intricate works is *After the Hunt in Scotland*, which was shown in silver after the Great Exhibition of 1851, and exhibits the

P. J. Mêne: *The Accolade*, 1852 (above), and *After the Hunt in Scotland*, 1861.

Polo players by
Isidore Bonheur, 1828.

influence of the painting of Sir Edwin Landseer. Although Mêne never visited England, probably as much of his work found its way across the Channel during the nineteenth century as remained in France. Almost all his works are of a sporting theme.

Isidore Bonheur (1827-1901) is another sculptor who produced some fine models (*see Plate 16*). His considerable talent has only been recognised comparatively recently, as the full extent of his work has come to light. He produced a wide variety of subjects, generally larger in size than those of his contemporaries, and always of fine quality – often cast by his uncle, Hippolyte Peyrol. Very little is known about him, as his life was probably overshadowed by his more celebrated sister, who also sculpted. However her work was, without exception, only sheep and cattle. He also sculpted one of the earliest – and still the best – models of polo, *The Game of Polo*, in 1897.

Paul Comolera (1818–1897), Ferdinand Pautrot (1832–1874) and Jules Moigniez (1835–1894) were particularly well known for their models of birds; they attempted a wide range of species mostly in decorative, rather than sporting, format. Four more important *animaliers* were Emmanuel Fremiet (1824–1910), better known for his monumental sculpture; Paul Gayrard (1807–1855) who produced a rare model of a carriage horse; Alfred Dubucand (1828–1894), influenced in particular by the Orientalists (*see Plate 16*), and Le Comte du Passage (1838–1909) who sculpted several fine pieces, often fairly large, including his fine model *Two Greyhounds Chasing a Hare*.

Despite the centre of sporting painting at this time being in England, surprisingly little sculpture in a similar vein was being produced, even though, as shown by the success of P. J. Mêne's work, there was an obvious demand for it. It was not until 1870 that one highly talented animal sculptor emerged, John Willis Good (1845–1879), but his bright promise was tragically cut short by suicide at the age of 34. Consequently, almost nothing is known about him other than

98

(above) *A Carriage Horse* by J. P. Gayrard, 1847, and (below) A bronze coursing study by Le Comte du Passage, c1870.

that he had a studio in London, in the Kings Road, studied briefly under J. E. Boehm, and exhibited at the Royal Academy from 1870 until his death. He produced about 20 models, almost all depicting racing or hunting, each modelled with infinite detail, yet also exuding great feeling. J. E. Boehm produced much fine sculpture, although little sporting in subject, but he did receive several commissions to sculpt leading racehorses of the day, in particular for Baron Rothschild.

It was left to Adrian Jones (1845–1938) to carry on the tradition in England and he produced a large number of highly competent models whose subjects were mainly drawn from the worlds of racing and foxhunting. Almost all his sculptures were portraits and were consequently cast in very small editions, normally in bronze, but occasionally in solid silver, as with the exceptional portrait of W. E. Oakley MFH on his favourite hunter, Icicle, given to him on his retirement as Master of the Atherstone.

There were several other sporting sculptors in England prior to the First World War, but, as their work was not popularised by the editing of large editions – unlike their French counterparts – they remained fairly obscure. Worth mentioning are Count Victor Gleichen (1833–1891) whose model of Edward VII in shooting dress in unusual; Cecil Brown (1868–1926), art master at Charterhouse, Joseph Durham (1814–1877), Oliver Wheatley (exhibited 1891–1920) and W. Roche (exhibited 1880–1911).

Mr W. E. Oakley riding Icicle and accompanied by some of his favourite hounds. A leaving present from the Atherstone hunt subscribers on his relinquishing the Mastership. The sculptor was Adrian Jones, 1890.

TRIMMER REGULUS W.E. OAKELEY M.F.H on ICICLE

100

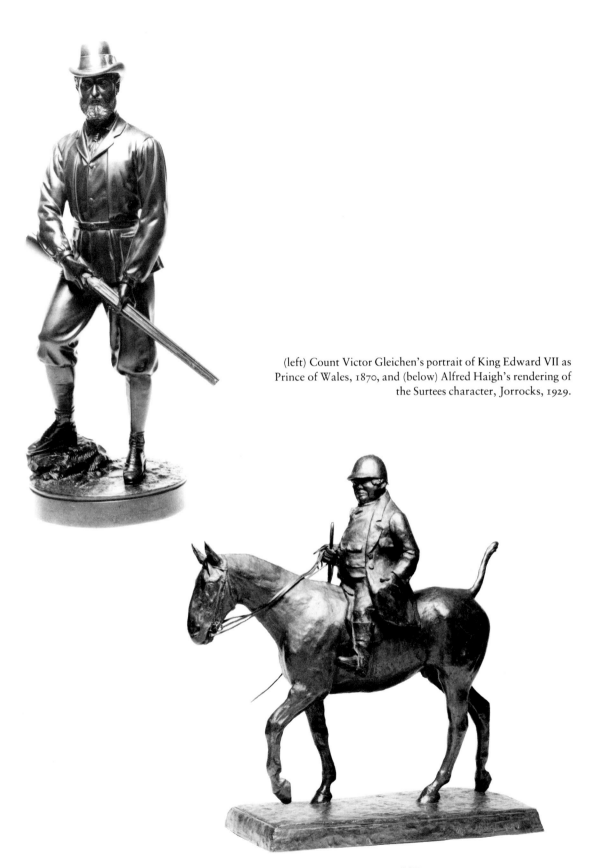

(left) Count Victor Gleichen's portrait of King Edward VII as
Prince of Wales, 1870, and (below) Alfred Haigh's rendering of
the Surtees character, Jorrocks, 1929.

As the nineteenth century drew to a close, the influence of Impressionism made itself felt on the sculptors of the day, and their work became looser, more sketchy, executed rapidly with little attention to detail. The champion of this new movement in sculpture was undoubtedly Rembrandt Bugatti, and although he confined himself mainly to animal subjects, executing very few models which could be described as a sporting subject, his influence was far-reaching. Towards the end of his life Edgar Dégas (1834–1917) turned almost exclusively to sculpture, concentrating mainly on female ballet dancers, but he also sculpted horses. He produced two or three horse-and-jockey compositions which show a development from the realistic models of the mid-nineteenth century. Shortly after the First World War there was another fine sculptor working in Paris, aptly called René Paris (born 1881). His work is, like Degas's, impressionistic, but it shows a greater understanding of the subject as well as a more confident handling of volume. He produced a few models, all of them excellent but, as they were edited in small numbers, they rarely appear on the market.

Herbert Haseltine (1877–1962) a highly talented artist, worked in a variety of styles and was strongly influenced by impressionism in his early pieces, as can be seen in his group *Polo Player – Riding Off*. He produced several portraits

Polo Players – Riding Off. A model by the American sculptor Herbert Haseltine, 1911.

The showjumper 'Stroller' with Marion
Coakes up, by Lorne McKean, c1970.

of racehorses, often with their jockeys, his bronze of *Spearmint* in the Racing
Museum, Saratoga, New York, being particularly fine. Although born in
America, he studied extensively in Europe, where he remained for most of his
life.

The immense popularity of the Art Nouveau, Art Deco and Arts and Crafts
movements, greatly reduced the amount of interest and demand for sporting
sculpture and, as a movement, it had all but died out by the beginning of the
Second World War.

It was John Skeaping (1901–1980) who, in the late 1960s, revived the interest.
As a young man he won the coveted *Prix de Rome* with work that was more
abstract in style, but horses and the sporting life in general always absorbed
him and became the focus of his attention for the last 20 years of his life. He
is perhaps best remembered for his ability to capture horses (and other animals)
in movement – both on canvas and in clay – and his early sculptures are more
impressionistic than his later work, possibly because he became occupied with
so many commissions from the early 1970s.

Many talented young animal artists such as Lorne McKean, Gill Wiles and Jonathon Kenworthy came on the scene in the 1970s, and today interest in, and demand for, sporting sculpture is probably at its strongest since its heyday in the second half of the nineteenth century. And now Britain – with sculptors such as Gill Parker, Emma MacDermott, Philip Blacker, Mark Coreth and Geoffrey Dashwood, among many others – leads the way.

For the established collector or first-time buyer, the field of sporting models has never been richer or more varied. There are still many fine and original examples of nineteenth century sculpture available, with some of the smaller pieces starting at £300–£400, although a good horse bronze by Mêne or Bonheur will be £3,000–£4,000 or more, depending on the model and its rarity.

The more impressionistic models from the turn of the century can cost considerably more than their nineteenth-century counterparts (size for size). However, for the keen collector with a good eye, some particularly good buys are still to be found from this period, especially by lesser or relatively unrecognised sculptors. The contemporary field offers a wide variety of styles and subjects to choose from, and here price is usually based on two things. Firstly, the talent and fame of the artist concerned, and secondly, the complexity of the model, and hence the relative cost of casting. Today the casting costs represent a far higher proportion of the selling price than they did 100 years ago, mainly because in those days labour was the cheapest commodity, whereas today it is the most expensive. Consequently, in order to reduce the labour costs, many foundries skimp on

Gill Parker's *Steeplechasers*, 1986.

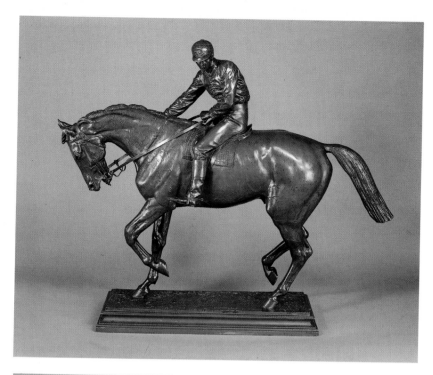

PLATE 16   (*above*) Study of a horse and jockey by Isidore Bonheur, *c* 1870.

(*below*) Arab hunter in bronze by A. Dubucand, *c* 1880.

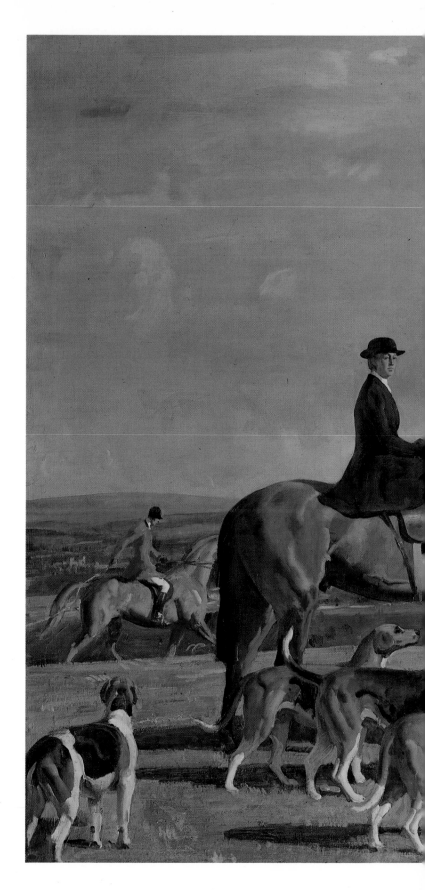

PLATE 17   A typical hunting conversation piece
by A. J. Munnings, 1920. It is of John J.
Moubray, Master of the Bedale foxhounds with
his wife, huntsman and whipper-in. The picture
was sold at Christie's in June 1986 for £300,000.

PLATE 18 *Riding to the Last* by Lionel Edwards, 1938. 'To give the impression of speed,' said Edwards, 'requires a lot of wangling!'

A Day's Bag by Jules Moigniez, *c*1870.

the labour intensive elements – generally the finishing or chasing of the bronzes – and it is this that will make the difference between a fine and an average quality casting.

Most original nineteenth-century bronzes are of good or fine quality, while the twentieth-century copies of them are poor, because the forgers do not take the time to finish them properly. It makes good sense to buy the best that one can afford, as the mediocre or fake is always difficult and sometimes impossible to re-sell. If in doubt, consult a specialist. That is what we are here for.

George Stubbs: *The Farmer's Wife and the Raven*, 1786, which changed
hands for 38 guineas in 1891.

6

AN AUCTIONEER'S VIEWPOINT

HENRY WYNDHAM

Educated at Eton and the Sorbonne, Henry Wyndham then completed
the Sotheby's fine arts course in London. He joined Christie's in 1974,
starting in the Old Master Department. Four years later he went to New York to
run Christie's Nineteenth-century Picture Department. In 1981 he
masterminded the specialist sales of sporting paintings, which have
since become one of the auctioneer's annual events.
In 1982 Henry Wyndham returned to London to head the Victorian Paintings
Department, but his particular interest in sporting art has never diminished,
especially in the work of George Stubbs and Sir Alfred Munnings.
In 1985 he became head of the Modern British Department – until 1987 when he
left Christie's to set up independently as an art dealer and consultant.

This fishing scene was painted jointly by Alfred Corbould and
H. L. Rolfe in 1862.

Nowadays, we are constantly hearing of record-breaking prices in the salerooms. Until ten years ago only a handful of pictures had broken the million pound barrier, but now hardly a month goes by without yet another work of art selling for seven or even eight figures. It has to be said that the majority of these tend to be Impressionist, Modern or Old Masters; however it was only recently that Stubbs's *Baron de Robeck on a Bay Cob* sold for $2.2 million in New York. Although the average sporting painting normally sells for considerably less, the 1980s have given rise to a dramatic surge of interest from new collectors. This has in turn forced prices up to unprecedented levels.

There are several reasons for this growing popularity, both in the salerooms and in galleries. Firstly, in the 1970s the British Sporting Art Trust was founded to further the interest of sporting art in this country. Secondly, exhibitions such as the British Sporting Painting Exhibition (1650–1850) at the Hayward Gallery in 1975 and the highly acclaimed Stubbs exhibition at the Tate Gallery in 1985 have created great interest.

Also of considerable influence is the part played by Paul Mellon. Without doubt, he has been the dominant figure over the last 40 years, not only as a collector, as can be seen by the superb collection at Yale, but he has also been very supportive in the setting up of the British Sporting Art Trust. In fact, he has been a major source of inspiration for collectors and enthusiasts throughout the world.

Besides all this exposure in the galleries, articles and books have been published on the subject, and perhaps as a result of all these influences there has been a tremendous increase in activity in the salerooms, with prices 'going through the roof'. To accommodate this increase in demand, specialist sporting painting sales have now become a regular feature.

The majority of sporting paintings to come up for sale in the English salerooms are from country houses. More often than not they represent a small part of a collection formed several generations before, containing Dutch and Italian old masters and English family portraits. However, there has also existed the purely sporting art collection, normally formed by one individual, and in some cases these eventually find their way into the saleroom, due to a death or the need to raise money.

One such example of an individual collector was Sir Walter Gilbey who founded the well-known wine merchants bearing his name. Besides this, he wrote numerous books and articles on agriculture, horse breeding and sporting subjects, such as *The Life of George Stubbs*, *Poultry Keeping on Farms and Small Holdings*, and *Horse Breeding in England and India*. His collection was sold in three parts. The first part was held in May 1891, and comprised paintings, drawings and prints from his country seat, Elsenham Hall. The 358 lots totalled just under £2,000 with the top price of 48 guineas for a George Morland of sheep. Part two, sold in March 1910, included 425 lots from Cambridge House, his residence in Regent's Park, which sold for just over £11,000. The sale included the two famous Sawrey Gilpins of *Voyage to the Houyhnhnms*, (Mellon Collection), which sold for 36 and 38 guineas, respectively.

Besides numerous works by Marshall, Seymour, Wootton, Ferneley and Herring, among others, there were 10 works by George Stubbs. They included *The Farmer's Wife and the Raven* (38 guineas) *Zebra in a Wood* (24 guineas) and *White Horse Frightened by a Lion* (21 guineas). In the same sale, pictures by William Shayer were selling for nearly £200 and watercolours by Charles Cooper Henderson, the coaching artist, for up to £70, three times as much as the average Stubbs.

The third sale was held after Gilbey's death in June 1915, and was made up of the remaining contents of Elsenham Hall, near Bishop's Stortford. It took seven days and totalled £28,000, of which 128 lots of sporting paintings were knocked down for over £18,000. Once again, Stubbs featured prominently with

The Chace, a mezzotint by T. Burford after James Seymour, 1787.

27 works. These included *Gimcrack with John Pratt* (220 guineas) – a sum approaching £750,000 was raised in 1982 to purchase it for the Fitzwilliam Museum, Cambridge; a *Stallion and Mare*, previously called *Jupiter* (10 guineas) which sold at Christie's, London, in July 1987 for £390,000; *Horses Fighting* (17 guineas), *Eclipse* (410 guineas) both now in the Mellon Collection; *The Haymakers* (420 guineas) and *The Reapers* (420 guineas). Also included was Reinagle and Gilpin's portrait of the legendary Colonel Thornton, with his twelve barrelled rifle (160 guineas) which sold again in 1983 for £68,000.

Besides all the most important artists, the sale also contained 24 paintings by George Morland. These latter works consistently made the highest prices, with *The Cottage Door* making 1,300 guineas and 1,150 guineas for *The Dram*, which ironically sold for only £3,800 as recently as 1982, a substantial loss in real terms. This is a classic case of changing fashion and reappraisal. Today it is hard to understand why secondary artists such as Morland and Shayer were held in such high esteem in relation to Stubbs, Marshall, Herring and Ferneley.

Perhaps the most important collection of all to come on the market was that of Walter Hutchinson, the publisher. The collection was formed over a fairly

A coursing scene by J. N. Sartorius, 1816.

Henry Alken's Leicestershire hunting scene, c1830, and (below) *Full Cry*,
a similar scene in the same country by John Ferneley Snr, 1825.

short space of time by Hutchinson and became the National Gallery of British Sports and Pastimes. Derby House, in Stratford Place, was acquired to house the collection and was consequently renamed Hutchinson House. Interestingly enough, some of the paintings had been acquired there when Christie's moved in during the war, from 1941. Regrettably, Walter Hutchinson died suddenly in 1950, intestate, and the collection went to auction in three parts between June 1951 and 1952. In all, 583 lots were sold for £135,000.

Apart from the £44,000 paid for Constable's *Flatford Mill* (which was recently sold to the nation in lieu of death duties for £10 million) the top price was 12,000 guineas for the magnificent Stubbs of *Gimcrack near the Rubbing House at New-market* (private collection) which would be worth a substantial sum today. Another Stubbs already featured in the Gilbey 1910 sale was *The Farmer's Wife and the Raven* (250 guineas). *Turf with Jockey Up* is another (5,000 guineas), which also now hangs in the Mellon Collection. However, most of the Stubbses sold for under £1,000, whereas two George Morlands went for over £5,000 each,

Lord Clermont's pointer bitch, Phyllis, painted by John Best in 1772. The painting was in the collection of Lady Forteviot and subsequently in that of Sir Walter Gilbey, who mistakenly believed it was a Stubbs.

113

considerably more than Hogarth's *Children Building a House of Cards* which made a modest 1,700 guineas. The sale also included 17 paintings by the then contemporary artist, Sir Alfred Munnings. His prices ranged from 1,500 guineas for *The Saddling Paddock, Cheltenham* to *The White Canoe*, which sold for 70 guineas. A similar painting sold at auction, in 1986, for £120,000. Wootton, Herring and Ferneley did not create much interest and generally sold for under £100 and in some instances for under £10.

In more recent times, the most important sale was undoubtedly the Jack Dick collection which was sold in four parts between 1973 and 1976. It contained nearly 200 lots, of all the most important sporting artists, but was particularly well represented with works by Herring, Ferneley and Pollard. Apart from Part two which suffered from the effects of the oil crisis, prices for these artists reached new levels, and the sale totalled just under £3 million.

Once again Stubbs was the top performer with £225,000 for *Goldfinder* and £170,000 for *The Duke of Grafton's Stallion, Mares and Foals*. James Pollard's *Trafalgar Square* sold for the then staggering price of £54,000. J. F. Herring's *Vespa, Held by Her Owner, Sir Mark Wood* sold for £62,000 in 1973 (*see Plate 19*), and a similar version sold in 1987 for £100,000. This theoretically represents a very small increase and in real terms actually a loss over 15 years, proving that not all works of art have appreciated at the same pace over the last 15 years. Another example of this is a fine Morland entitled *Feeding Pigs* which sold for only £5,000. Judging by what has already been said, this would have made considerably more in real terms 60 years earlier. On the other hand, Marshall's *Bravura*, which made £16,000 in Part two, sold for £240,000 in 1986. Overall, the majority of Herring's and Ferneley's averaged below £10,000. It was really not until the early 1980s that prices for these artists took off.

During the 1980s, two notable collections have come on the market. First, the Harry Peters Collection in New York in 1982, with its interesting group of paintings by Arthur Fitzwilliam Tait, the American artist, not to mention works by Stubbs, Sartorius and Boultbee, among others. And then, in 1984, the Joel Collection was sold at Christie's in London. Although only 24 lots, the sale totalled over £3.6 million. The highlight was *The Doncaster Gold Cup* (1838) by Herring and Pollard, which was knocked down for £720,000. This same painting made 900 guineas at a sale in 1943. Other strong prices included £320,000 paid for Herring's *Preparing to Start for the Doncaster Gold Cup, 1825* (*see Plate 20*), and £200,000 for Ferneley's *The Cur* (*see Plate 5*).

Aside from these rather infrequent single-owner sales, there has always been a steady supply of sporting paintings in the salerooms, normally making up part of a sale, along with portraits, landscapes and marine pictures. Then, in 1981, Christie's began their annual specialist sporting painting sales in New York. These have been enormously successful over the years, proving that this is one of the most widely collected fields in the art world today.

Besides London and New York, sporting paintings turn up in country sales. And, as recently as 1986, several paintings by Stubbs were discovered, including

A Son of Old Sterling by George Stubbs, *c*1765.

A Son of Old Sterling, bought in a country sale for under £1,000, and sold, within a few months, in New York for over £250,000. Also two small paintings of foxhounds, bought in the country for a few hundred pounds, sold a few months later for nearly £100,000. But these discoveries have become less and less frequent.

The market today is still formidable at the top level, as proven by the $2.2 million paid for Stubbs's *Baron de Robeck on a Bay Cob* mentioned above. But, although there are plenty of sporting pictures available, very few are of the top quality. As a result the market has tended to be swamped with rather over-priced second-rate pictures. This was exemplified by nearly 700 paintings available in New York over two days in June 1987. Indications are that it has noticeably softened especially for the second rate and lower end of the market.

It is also worth noting that the decline in the prices for sporting art has coincided with the fall in bloodstock prices. This comes as no surprise, as many buyers of bloodstock collect sporting paintings.

The demand for Munnings has definitely tailed off, except for his more important works, as exemplified by the six feet wide 'Start' which recently sold for over $1 million. The rather overpriced lesser works by Munnings which have recently flooded the market are now difficult to sell. The demand for decorative and sentimental paintings is not quite as strong as it was. However, although the tremendous surge of the early 1980s has levelled off, one is surprised every now and again by exceptional prices. One trend that has been noticeable is the re-cycling of pictures. Frequently the same picture turns up again in the saleroom within a relatively short space of time.

The majority of today's buyers come from America, hence the inauguration

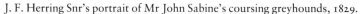

J. F. Herring Snr's portrait of Mr John Sabine's coursing greyhounds, 1829.

Friedrich Wilhelm Keyl's portrait of Mr and Mrs Sam Gurney at
Culver, Carshalton, 1851.

of the annual New York sales. The buyers can be categorised as follows. Firstly
there is the dedicated collector who has studied the subject very carefully and
buys very selectively. Then there is the less sophisticated collector who has probably never bought pictures before but happens to be a racing or hunting enthusiast and just likes to be surrounded by horses. And lastly, there is the one-off
buyer who has a space to fill on his wall, and is looking for a decorative picture
to fit in with the interior decoration. This group tends to buy the dog pictures
and is generally unconcerned by the artist.

To any prospective collector I would offer these words of advice. As in any
field with which you are unfamiliar, whether stocks or shares, property or wine,
never be afraid to take advice. A lot of money can be at stake and there are
many traps in which the amateur can become ensnared. For instance there are
a considerable number of fakes in circulation. Of course, whether these paintings
were originally painted to deceive, one will never know. In many cases signatures
have been added at a later date, or attributions changed, perhaps in good faith.
However, always be sure that what you are buying is the genuine article; most
reputable galleries and auction houses give guarantees of authenticy. Therefore,
try to stick to the well-known organisations when buying and you will not go
far wrong.

Artists such as Herring were frequently faked and imitated, and just occasionally it can be difficult even for the experts to tell. Over the last few years there

has been some dispute over certain paintings which have previously been cata-
logued as Herring Snr and are now thought to be by his son. Landseer, too,
is an artist who is frequently imitated, and the difference in price between genuine
and fake is considerable. And it is surprising how even the minor artists are
faked, or have suspect signatures. If you are worried, always check the signature
under ultra-violet light. Although not foolproof it can be of great help. If in
any doubt consult a reputable expert, and be prepared to pay him a fee; it will
pay dividends in the end.

Two final words of advice, always buy what you like and buy the best quality
that you can afford and do not be seduced by name. In other words try to buy
a really good example of an artist. For £30,000 you could buy a Stubbs, but
the chances are that it will be a fairly moderate example, to say the least. However, for the same money you could buy an extremely good quality painting
by Sartorius or Barenger, which, apart from anything else, will tend to be a
better investment, although that should never be the reason for buying a picture.

What then of the future? I believe that the finest pictures will continue to
make strong prices, while the lesser works will fluctuate according to the state
of the art market as a whole. One area, however, I do see with growth potential

On the Way to the Meet by George Wright, *c*1900.

118

Epsom by Gilbert Holiday, 1933.

in the long term is the so far rather neglected twentieth-century British sporting art. Apart from Munnings and to a lesser extent Lionel Edwards, they are relatively unknown, especially abroad, and still reasonably cheap. I think we shall be hearing more about artists such as Gilbert Holiday, Basil Nightingale and John Skeaping among others, over the next few years. Time will tell.

Sawrey Gilpin's *Gulliver taking his final leave in the Land of the Houyhnhnms*, *c*1768. This picture forms part of the Paul Mellon Collection at the Yale Center for British Art.

PLATE 19 (*above*) *Vespa, held by her owner, Sir Mark Wood*, painted by J. F. Herring Snr, 1833. The horse's trainer leans on the stable door while a groom holds the owner's hack.

(*left*) *The Blacksmith's Shop* by J. F. Herring Snr, 1856. This picture was lent from a private collection to the British Sporting Art Trust, in whose Vestey gallery at Newmarket it now hangs.

PLATE 20   *Preparing to start for the Doncaster Gold Cup, 1825,*
by J. F. Herring Snr.

PLATE 21   (*above*) *Fishing on the Stour at Stratford Mill*, by John Constable, 1820.
(*below*) A portrait by J. F. Lewis of Sir Edwin Landseer, accompanied by his ghillie, 1830.

7

GREAT COLLECTORS

AMANDA KAVANAGH

After graduating from the Courtauld Institute, where she read history
of art, Amanda Kavanagh worked as an archivist at the
Paul Mellon Center for Studies in British Art from 1982 to 1985.
Since 1986 she has been working as librarian, picture researcher and
cataloguer at the Richard Green Gallery in Dover Street, London,
specialists in animal and sporting art. She has contributed to
both *Country Life* and *The Antique Collector*.

John Kent, trainer to the Duke of Richmond on Newmarket Heath by
J. F. Herring Snr, 1831. The painting is one of those on loan to the Tate
Gallery sporting room.

Collectors of sporting art have rarely been considered connoisseurs, partly through prejudice, and partly because the genre developed outside the mainstream of European art. Sporting pictures evolved out of an essentially English tradition of country life and leisure, and in particular, an enthusiasm for hunting, shooting, fishing and racing. These were the favoured sports of the landed gentry, the first patrons of sporting art, in whose homes many of the best collections still remain as a permanent pictorial tribute 'to the best of England, recorded in the best English way'.[1]

It was perhaps more sport than art that led to Sir Walter Gilbey's volumes of *Animal Painters* (1900), an exercise continued by Walter Shaw Sparrow later in the 1920s. Such efforts prompted the critic Ellis Waterhouse to remark that, 'To discuss the Sartorius tribe and such painters is no business of the historian of art no matter how bitter the accusations of neglect are wont to be from those specialist writers who sometimes confuse the history of art with praising famous horses'.[2]

Many fine collections of sporting art are still to be found in historic houses, acquired through successive generations as part of a family heritage. Such strongholds of artistic talent and national history reveal an important aspect of English patronage, and indicate the documentary value of sporting art. As Oliver Millar said in *British Sporting Painting (1650–1850)*[3]: 'If we are prepared to devote study to a collection of family portraits in the hall of a country house ... we cannot logically ignore the record the same patron may have commissioned of the animals in his stable and their breeding.'

One of the most important private collectors of sporting art at the end of the nineteenth, and beginning of the twentieth century was Lord Woolavington (1849–1939), who assembled his pictures at Lavington Park in Sussex. To this collection, the late Sir Reginald and Lady Macdonald-Buchanan (Lord Woolavington's daughter) made considerable additions, now all housed at Cottesbrooke Hall, Northamptonshire. Included in this collection are pictures of a general rural theme, apart from those more specifically devoted to sport, of which a group by Ben Marshall is an impressive feature.

An innate personal interest in sport inspired many collectors, among whom Sir Walter Gilbey must rank as one of the most illustrious. The significance of his collection at Elsenham Hall in Hertfordshire was widely recognised, and shortly before the major part of his collection was sold by Christie's in June, 1915, *Baily's Magazine* commented: 'The dispersal this month of the late Sir Walter Gilbey's remarkably fine collection of sporting, hunting and other

Goldfinder by George Stubbs, 1774. Formerly in Jack Dick's collection, it was
sold at auction for £225,000.

pictures and engravings of open-air life in Great Britain will be the most important event of its kind held during the last 40 or 50 years. In a sense the sale will
be a matter of regret, for it means the scattering of the gatherings of a long
lifetime of an acknowledged authority, the breaking up of a collection, which
has formed the basis of many indispensable books of reference.'

Sporting collections of a more specialised nature were often the outcome of
single-minded devotion to one chosen field, and certain collectors therefore
became synonymous with particular sports. The name of Arthur Gilbey will
always be associated with angling, and 'certainly no angler went to greater pains
to gather round him precious works and literature bearing on his absorbing
sport.'[4] Likewise, H. J. Joel, (b. 1892), known as Jim Joel, one of the greatest
English owner–breeders, acquired many sporting pictures that reflect his lifelong

devotion to the Turf, many of which were sold by Christie's in July 1984.

The growing realisation, from the 1920s onwards, that 'no public gallery in England does justice to sporting painters ... and ... what we all need, in fact, is a National Gallery of British Empire Sports',[5] prompted several collectors to establish such a collection. In 1936 a room was set aside at the Tate Gallery entirely for sporting paintings. Its existence depended primarily on loans from the private collections of Mrs Carstairs and H. Arthurton, and although it was intended to maintain 'a nucleus of pictures in the permanent collection, and a constantly changing series of works from private sources'[6], the room had closed within a year.

A serious endeavour took place in 1949, when Walter Hutchinson, the famous publisher and printer, founded the National Gallery of British Sports and Pastimes, at Derby House, Stratford Place, where he exhibited 618 works from his collection, comprising over 3,000 paintings and prints. An article in the *Burlington Magazine*, April 1949, commented upon 'the importance of Mr

The End of the Day's Shoot by J. F. Herring Snr, 1829. This painting which was in Walter Hutchinson's collection, was subsequently bought by Jack Dick.

125

Hutchinson's gesture in throwing open to the public his national gallery of British Sports and Pastimes'[7], but the collection was also criticised elsewhere for 'over-crowding . . . and above all for the confusion of thought and aims which has led to the inclusion of pictures . . . which have really nothing to do with sport at all.'[8] Ultimately it was financial difficulties which led to the sale of this collection at Christie's in 1951–2.

It took an enlightened American collector, Paul Mellon, to encourage the English to reappraise their own sporting paintings and he stated, 'It is a sad fact that British sporting art has been looked down on by the critics and the intelligentsia from the eighteenth century to the present day . . . but the best so-called sporting artists have always been able to hold their own technically and aesthetically with the best landscapists and portraitists of the day'.[9]

Ostensibly, his collection was to provide a survey of British art during its heyday, from 1700 to 1850, of which sporting paintings were the outstanding feature. Unlike his compatriot collectors, such as Frick, Huntington, and his father, Andrew Mellon, whose preference tended towards the grand tradition of formal portraiture, Paul Mellon showed a predilection for conversation pictures, landscapes and sporting subjects.

It was Mellon's unwavering belief that 'British sporting art has always blindly and mistakenly been grossly underrated,'[10] that determined him to found what was to be one of the finest collections to exist either in private or public ownership. Education played a predominant role in the formation of his aesthetic taste, and he readily admitted his 'tendency to think of my British collecting as the most enjoyable end product of my Yale and Cambridge days.'[11] At Yale he was taught above all to appreciate English history and literature, and that education, he said, 'pushed me further over the brink into a state of galloping Anglophilia

A racing group by John Skeaping, 1978. The collector, Paul Mellon, gave the bronze to the National Horseracing Museum, Newmarket.

126

David Dalby's portrait of the Arabian horse, Signal, 1829: from the
Paul Mellon collection.

– or perhaps I should say, I turned into a galloping Anglophile.' [12] His subsequent
years at Cambridge fostered his lifelong love of British sport and the countryside,
and he later recalled: 'I drank deeply of her scenery, her history, her life, her
sport, her beer ... I r-o-d-e constantly, I r-o-w-e-d intermittently, I r-e-a-d a
little ...' [13]

When Mellon married in 1935, his father gave him two of his best paintings
by Marshall and two by Sartorius as a wedding present. He then started buying
racing, hunting and other sporting paintings, and despite his father's denigration
of racing and hunting – and his much quoted dictum, 'Any damn fool knows one
horse can run faster than another,' Mellon bought his first racehorse at this time.

It was not until 1959, however, when he became chairman of the *Sport and
Horse* exhibition committee at the Virginia Museum of Fine Arts, that the collection began to be seriously assembled. Through this appointment he met Basil

The Reverend Thomas Levett out shooting by James Ward, 1811. The picture
was in Colonel R. G. Levett's collection.

Taylor, the distinguished art historian and critic, with whom he shared his enthusiasm for English art in general, and a special admiration for the work of Stubbs,
resulting in the best single collection of that artist's work.

Mellon formed the foundation of his collection between 1959 and 1963, the
year in which it was first exhibited at the Virginia Museum of Fine Arts, under
the title *Painting in England 1700–1850*. It was subsequently shown at the Royal
Academy, in 1964–65, and finally at Yale University Art Gallery in 1965. In 1966
Mellon decided to bequeath the greater part of his British collection to Yale
University and to provide funds for a building to house it. 'It seemed to me,'
he reasoned, 'that the ferment of a university would enliven and stimulate the
study of, and the enjoyment of, these artistic relics of our British inheritance,
more vitally and more resourcefully than if they were passively displayed in a
non-teaching institution.'[14] Known as the Yale Center for British Art, the building was opened in 1977. He also donated a fine selection of his sporting pictures

to the Virginia Museum of Fine Arts, housed in the new West Wing, which he also helped to finance, in 1985.

Mellon stimulated interest in a field in which there appeared a number of rivals, of which Jack Dick, was probably the most notable. Dick had built up from nothing a multi-million dollar business, Black Watch Farms, and formed a large collection of important sporting paintings. Both ventures proved short-lived, and serious financial difficulties made it imperative to sell his collection. Dick's business influenced the subject-matter of his paintings, and he began by collecting pictures of cattle. He was at this time, in his own words, 'the leading breaker of Arabian horses in the United States,' and this interest prompted him to purchase pictures of Arab horses. Through these preoccupations he became familiar with a wider range of sporting art, and, during the 1960s, competed strongly in the salerooms to secure the best available works.

The dispersal of Dick's collection took place in four sales at Sotheby's, London, between 1973 and 1976. Preceded by weeks of controversial and trans-atlantic litigation, the first sale provoked exceptional interest and sensational prices. As *The Times* correspondent noted, 'Prices went through the roof . . . Stubbs's *Goldfinder*, the star picture of the sale, fetched £225,000, an auction

A. F. Rolfe's *Three Anglers in a Punt*, 1856. The picture was formerly in the collection of Mrs Ambrose Clark.

129

record for England's greatest sporting artist. The painting went to Richard Green, the London dealer.'

Several other discerning collectors with a less public profile, likewise assembled valuable collections of sporting art. One of the more unusual collectors was Sir Abe Bailey, the South African mining magnate and racehorse owner, who died in 1940, and bequeathed his entire collection to the South African National Gallery. Although philanthropically intended for public display, the majority of these works were sadly destined for the dusty vaults of the museum, due to a shortage of space. The same fate befell the sporting paintings of Walter Stone, which were bequeathed to the Walker Art Gallery in Liverpool in 1938, but few of them see the light of day. It is through the foundation of the British Sporting Art Trust, in 1977, that major works from the collections of Mellon and Ambrose Clark were donated to the Tate Gallery, some of which are now displayed in the BSAT's Gallery at the National Horseracing Museum, Newmarket, which was opened in 1986.

Perhaps the most important prerequisites of the collector are pure pleasure, derived from acquisition, and a 'desire to own, to enjoy, to savour and to conserve rare and beautiful things'.[15] It is for such reasons that the greatest collections of sporting art have been assembled by private collectors rather than public institutions, and it is of some relevance to recall the famous words from the will of Edmond de Goncourt, who declared it his wish that his prints, drawings, books and other curiosities should 'not be consigned to the cold tomb of a museum and subjected to the stupid glare of the careless passer-by,' but that they should be dispersed under the auctioneer's hammer, 'so that the pleasure which the acquiring of each one of them has given me shall be given again, in each case, to some inheritor of my own tastes.'

SOURCES

[1] *Sporting Pictures at Lavington Park.* The Right Hon. Lord Woolavington, introduction by Sir Theodore Cook, 1927.
[2] Ellis Waterhouse, *Painting in Britain 1530–1790*, 1953.
[3] Oliver Millar, *British Sporting Painting (1650–1850).* London, Arts Council of Great Britain, 1974–75.
[4] 'A Great Collection of Angling Pictures,' *The Field*, 13 April 1940.
[5] Walter Shaw Sparrow, *British Sporting Artists.* Bodley Head, 1922
[6] David Fincham, 'The Sporting Room at Millbank', *Apollo*, March 1931
[7] 'The National Gallery of British Sports and Pastimes', *Burlington Magazine*, April 1949.
[8] R. A. Bevan, 'Mr Hutchinson's Sporting Venture', *Image*, No 2, 1949.
[9] John Baskett, *The Horse in Art*, Foreword by Paul Mellon, 1980.
[10] Yale Center for British Art, *Selected Paintings, Drawings and Books*, Foreword by Paul Mellon, 'A Collector Recollects', 1977.
[11] *Ibid.*
[12] *Ibid.*
[13] *Ibid.*
[14] *Ibid.*
[15] Edmund D. Pilsbury, *Paul Mellon as Collector and Patron of British Art. Selected Painting Acquisitions 1976–1980*. Essays in honour of Paul Mellon, 1986.

8

THE SPORTING BOOK COLLECTOR

GREGORY WAY

Following a five-year apprenticeship in the antiquarian department of
the Cambridge firm W. Heffer and Sons, Gregory Way returned to Newmarket
to become a partner in his father's antiquarian bookshop.
R. E. and G. B. Way is one of the country's leading firms of antiquarian
booksellers. It specialises in books on equestrian
and field sports subjects.

The aquatint frontispiece to Edward Orme's *Collection of British Field Sports*, 1807–8.

The attraction of collecting illustrated sporting books is that the number that have been published over the years is so large that it is possible to build a collection at a price to suit the individual, and you do not necessarily have to spend large sums of money to have a collection. It is in fact still possible to collect illustrated sporting books for a fraction of the price of the prints by the same artist. This is particularly so with the works illustrated by twentieth-century artists, such as Lionel Edwards, 'Snaffles', Gilbert Holiday, Cecil Aldin and others. It may not be possible today to build up vast and highly valuable sporting libraries like those formed by C. F. G. R. Schwerdt, Paul Mellon, Marcel Jeanson and others, but it is still feasible to find books that were described as 'rare' in the 1920s.

A good example of this is Blome's *The Gentleman's Recreation*, (1686, second edition 1710), which was the first real attempt to publish an encyclopaedia of sports, as well as arts and science. This is pointed out by Schwerdt in his magnificent four-volume catalogue, published in 1928, as follows: 'It is not exactly rare, although often described as such, and we recommend its purchase to collectors now that the older sporting books are fast disappearing.' Copies of this important work can still be found today.

Another work that is scarce, but can still be found, is the Duke of Newcastle's *General System of Horsemanship*. It was published in England in 1743, having first appeared on the Continent. Published in two volumes – the first containing the 43 magnificent engravings of dressage, and the second being concerned with horsemastership – this book should be the cornerstone of any collection of English books on equitation.

Another work of great importance to the collector of horse books is George Stubbs's *Anatomy of the Horse* (1766). It is a remarkable work, not only for the fact it was so entirely correct, but also for the problems he must have had in working on the carcasses without the help of refrigeration. Bibliographically it was a difficult work, as the printers obviously had a large number of sheets for the text, but they kept reprinting the plates. Genuine first issues, with the plates unwatermarked with a date, are rare, but many copies sold as first editions are not. When looked at closely the plates can be identified as being as late as 1820.

It was in the first half of the nineteenth century that the golden age of hand-coloured sporting books appeared – with the works of Henry Alken Snr, Thomas Rowlandson, Samuel Howitt and others. The most prolific of those was Henry Alken Snr, a fine sportsman in his own right. The quality of his book illustrations, despite his prodigious output, are of the highest standard. Probably his finest

Hog hunters meeting by surprise a tigress and her cubs, from Thomas
Williamson's *Oriental Field Sports*. Published by E. Orme 1805–7.

work, *The National Sports of Great Britain*, was published in 1821. The first
issue has the engraved title page dated 1820, and Schwerdt tells us that it is
'exceptionally rare'. Many of Alken's other works are in a humorous vein. A
large number have been 'broken up' and framed, making nearly all of his books
difficult to find.

Edward Orme's *Collection of British Field Sports* (1807) is another example
of fine hand-coloured work. Schwerdt claims of this work that it is 'the finest
and most important sporting book of the last two centuries'. The plates are
by Samuel Howitt. A copy in original wrappers sold for £2,600 in 1928. The
same year Samuel Howitt illustrated Thomas Williamson's *Oriental Field
Sports*, the finest work in my opinion on Indian field sports. It was for many
years underrated (probably on account of its gory pictures), and has only, over
the last few years, been making the prices it should.

Sir William Cornwallis Harris published his *Wild Sports of Southern Africa*
in 1839. The first edition had no pictures, but the later ones are nicely illustrated;

the fifth edition, published in 1852, is regarded as the best. Harris also had published in 1840 his *Portraits of the Game and Wild Animals of Southern Africa*; this large folio is one of the finest works on African wildlife. In 1844 George Catlin published a portfolio of prints of *Hunting Scenes and Amusements of the Rocky Mountains and Prairies of America*. With its 25 fine plates copies are not easy to discover, particularly those in good condition.

These three works were the start of many publications on big game hunting. Among the best of them are the series published by Rowland Ward, and written by H. A. Bryden, under the title *The Great and Small Game of Africa*, and Richard Lydekker's *Great and Small Game of India, Wild Oxen, Sheep and Goats, The Deer of all Lands* and *The Great and Small Game of Europe*. This series was limited to printings of 500 or 250 copies, and finely illustrated by W. Kuhnert and others. They were published between 1898 and 1901.

There were not many fine early nineteenth century illustrated shooting books

A coloured lithograph from *The Hunter's Annual*, published by A. H. Baily, 1836. By G. W. Giles, after R. B. Davis, the subject is T. Goosey, huntsman to the Belvoir.

published. In 1804 Thornhill's *Shooting Directory* was issued, with both coloured and uncoloured plates. Pages 215–220 contained the *Come the old Soldier* passage, an account of how the Government tried to obtain Joseph Manton's rifling invention. (In the second issue these pages were removed.)

In 1837 Lawrence Rawstone wrote his *Gamonia*, or the *Art of Preserving Game*, containing 15 very highly finished coloured plates. Peter Hawker's *Instructions to Young Sportsmen* first appeared in 1814. This was published anonymously, without any illustrations and is a rare book; it is the third edition, with its coloured plates, that is the most attractive.

During the nineteenth century several other sporting subjects produced some very attractive books. For example, in the sphere of coaching, C. E. Newhouse's *Scenes of the Road* (1834–5) and *The Roadsters Annual* (1845), are very rare, mostly due to the fact that many copies have been broken up for their illustrations. Towards the second half of the nineteenth century the Jorrocks novels of R. S. Surtees were printed. Originally, they were published in monthly parts, with illustrations mainly by John Leech and 'Phiz' (Hablot K. Browne). Sets of the five novels that appeared in the original parts are rare, mainly because they were only intended as a magazine, and not bound to last. It is also difficult to discover the first-bound editions in original cloths in good condition, but later

An aquatint by Charles Rosenberg after J. L. Agasse: *The Road-Side*, 1833.

Some of the Right Sort doing the Thing Well, a lithograph
by Henry Alken, 1821–2.

editions are to be found. They hold a place of their own in English sporting
literature of the nineteenth century.

Another popular work of the nineteenth century was Charles James
Apperley's (Nimrod's) *The Life of the Late John Mytton*, first published in 1835
with 12 colour plates by Alken. The first edition in original cloth in good condition is very rare. It went into a second edition in 1837, with 18 coloured plates.
Two plates were replaced from the first edition as they were considered too
bloodthirsty, and eight extra plates were produced, mainly by T. J. Rawlins.
Nimrod also wrote another fine work, *The Life of a Sportsman*. The first issue
was published in blue cloth, the second issue in red cloth.

A work highly esteemed in the nineteenth century was William Scrope's *The
Art of Deerstalking*. First published in 1838, with plates by Edwin and Charles
Landseer, the book shows how the sport was carried out with the aid of
deerhounds before modern rifles were introduced. Scrope's other most famous
work was *Days and Nights of Salmon Fishing in the Tweed*.

137

A lithographic frontispiece by Henry Alken for a series on the Duke of Beaufort's hunt: *The Sportsman's Arms*, published by Thomas McLean, 1833, and (below) *Crossing the River Avon*, an aquatint from the same series.

There were, too, some very important periodicals produced in the nineteenth century. The most significant of these was *The Sporting Magazine*. First produced in 1793 it continued until 1870, illustrated throughout with steel engraved plates. It is a tragedy that so many sets have been broken up for their plates, as it is the outstanding piece of its time, with nearly all the best authors of the period writing it, and thus the most useful source of information for sports of that time. Sets of the 156 volumes are now rare, and, I think, still under-valued when they do come on the market. Another periodical published between 1822 and 1828 was *The Annals of Sporting and Fancy Gazette*. The early volumes were illustrated with fine handcoloured, as well as black-and-white, plates. The last issue, published in June 1828, is said to be the most rare, so much so that a copy changed hands for $500 in 1910.

At the end of the nineteenth century and into the twentieth century two other magazines were published, *Baily*'s and *The Badminton*. They contain many interesting articles by the best authors of the day, sometimes on some quite unusual diversions (e.g. *Big Game Hunting from a Camel*, and *Duck Shooting in the Himalayas*). *The Badminton Magazine* led to the publishing of the 'Badminton Library' series with volumes on a variety of subjects from *Big Game Hunting* to *Motors*.

For many years the handcoloured and steel-engraved plate books from the nineteenth century and earlier have only been valued at their price per illustra-

One of a series from *The Young English Foxhunter*. An aquatint by Charles Hunt after F. C. Turner, 1841.

THE YOUNG ENGLISH FOX HUNTER.

THE DESSERT

tion, and a large number of them have been broken up, which is a pity if only because many of the handcoloured plates that are framed soon lose their colours when exposed to strong light for even quite a short period.

For a collector of these coloured-plate works it is always better to buy a good copy of the book, with nice colouring, and without off-setting (when the ink comes off the printed page and can be seen on the coloured plate). This usually happened when the publishers did not insert a tissue leaf between the printed page and the coloured plate. Some books are particularly prone to this; a good example is Alken's *National Sports*, where it can be very noticeable. After the last quarter of the nineteenth century, the problem of condition of the plates does not arise so much, as most coloured plates were printed in colour, rather than handcoloured.

Once into the twentieth century the field of illustrated sporting books becomes enormous, since most of the best painters also produced book illustrations, and there were more books produced.

It is possible to build quite a large collection by only collecting the works of one artist or author. Authors like Lionel Edwards and Cecil Aldin either wrote or illustrated well over 100 works each. Some of the nicest reproductions were those done for the works of Archibald Thorburn. His *British Birds*, first published in 1915–16, for example, is a fine work and it is more desirable if you can find it with the two supplementary plates, issued separately in wrappers. Other works illustrated by Thorburn were *British Mammals* (1920–21), *A Naturalist's Sketchbook* (1919) and *Game Birds and Wildfowl* (1923); the reproductions in these are of better quality than nearly anything published today. Edmund Caldwell is best known for his illustrations in *Jock of the Bushveld* written by Sir Percy Fitzpatrick, but it is difficult to find a copy in a first edition.

Other fine pieces of book production published at the same period were the series *Gun at Home and Abroad*, four volumes, *Racing at Home and Abroad*, three volumes, *Fishing at Home and Abroad*, and *Polo at Home and Abroad*. They were illustrated by many of the best artists of the day, including George Lodge, A. Thorburn, E. Caldwell, and V. Balfour Browne.

Other illustrators of big game hunting books include J. G. Millais, who wrote and illustrated – among several other naturalist classics – *A Breath from the Veldt*, being the observations of a naturalist-artist in South Africa. His folio works were badly bound in their original editions, because the publishers used a rubber solution, instead of stitching the pages. This means that when the books are opened today, the binding is likely to break, as the rubber solution, having dried out, is brittle.

Although George Lodge did do a number of illustrations of big game books, he is best known for his illustrations of birds, particularly birds of prey and falconry. His *Memoirs of an Artist Naturalist* is an interesting and readable work. Other artists who are best known for their illustrations of birds include Philip Rickman, whose *Selection of Bird Paintings and Sketches*, published in a limited edition of 475 copies in 1979, shows that it is still possible to produce

Illustrations by John Leech from the Surtees novels:
(above) 'Mr Sponge's Red Coat commands no
Respect' from *Mr Sponge's Sporting Tour*, 1852,
and (right) 'Caught in the Rain' from *Ask Mama*,
1857. (below) A later illustrator of Surtees: Cecil
Aldin, 1912.

G. D. Armour: 'Goal!', a sketch from his
autobiographical *Bridle and Brush*, 1937, and (right) an
illustration for a front cover of *Country Life* during the
1920s.

a fine modern book if enough trouble is taken. His earlier works contain some charming pencil sketches.

J. C. Harrison's *Birds of Prey of the British Isles* published in 1980 in a limited edition of 275 copies, is not as well produced as the work by Rickman, and although it is a nice book it was overpriced when published. Other natural history and sporting illustrators who are very collectable at the present time include 'B.B.' (D. J. Watkins-Pitchford) and C. F. Tunnicliffe who illustrated works on a large number of country subjects.

In the sphere of twentieth-century illustrated works on hunting, one artist stands out for the quality as well as the quantity of his book illustrations and that is Lionel Edwards. The first work he illustrated was A. E. H. Alderson's *Pink and Scarlet* or *Hunting as a School for Soldiering* (1913). Edwards's publications, *My Scottish Sketchbook* (1929), *My Hunting Sketchbook* (2 vols., 1928–30), *My Irish Sketchbook* (1938) and *A Leicestershire Sketchbook* (1935) are among his best known and most popular of the great host of his works. A number of his books were published as limited editions as well as general editions; the most desirable of those, perhaps, was *The Passing Seasons*, limited to 250 copies,

Co-ops from *A Half Century of Memories* by 'Snaffles', 1949, shows his impression of *nouveaux riches* at a shoot.

143

with each of the 18 plates signed by the artist, and *A Sportsman's Bag*, again with 18 plates, each signed, but this was limited to 100 copies. That made a total of 6,300 plates signed by him in those two works alone.

Cecil Aldin's first work *Spot, an Autobiography* (a dog story) was published in 1894 and nearly all his early works were children's books. Many of them are now hard to find, particularly in good condition, mainly because of the handling they received from children.

Sir Alfred Munnings only produced one major illustrated sporting book; *Pictures of Horses and English Life*. It was first published in 1927 in a general edition, and in a limited edition of 250 signed copies. It was revised and reissued in 1939. Other important twentieth-century sporting book illustrators include Gilbert Holiday, whose *Horses and Soldiers* published privately in 1939 is a lovely book of illustrations of the military side of horsemanship, particularly the Royal Horse Artillery. Then there is F. A. Stewart, whose three major illustrated works are *Hark to the Hounds* (1937), *Cross Country with Hounds* (1936) and *Hunting Countries* (1935), all published in a similar oblong format.

'Snaffles' (C. J. Payne) is an immensely popular artist today. Many of his early book illustrations are of life in India, particularly in *My Sketchbook in the Shiny* (1930), and *More Bandobast* (1936). But *'Osses and Obstacles* (1935) proves to be his most popular book. He also wrote and illustrated *A Half Century of Memories* (1940), *Four-Legged Friends and Acquaintances* (1951) and *I've Heard the Revelly* (1953).

9

THE BRITISH
SPORTING ART TRUST

ROBERT FOUNTAIN

By profession a medical practitioner, Robert Fountain's abiding private
interest has always been sporting art, an interest first aroused by his cousin,
Hugh McClausland, of coaching fame. In 1972 Robert Fountain became a
founder-member of the British Sporting Art Trust and the Trust's first
honorary secretary. In 1982 he was elected executive chairman.
He was also, at one time, honorary secretary of the Burton Hunt, of which
he remains an active supporter.
Starting, in 1968, with an article entitled 'The Anatomical Work of
George Stubbs', in *The Proceedings of the Royal Society of Medicine*, he has
written extensively on sporting art. He was co-author, with Alfred Gates,
of *Stubbs's Dogs*, which was published in 1986.

Two Hunters with a Groom, painted in about 1805 by J. L. Agasse. One of the paintings given by Paul Mellon to the British Sporting Art Trust, and now hanging in the Tate Gallery.

To the serious collector of sporting art the location of reference works is often important and usually of interest. Until recently all they could do was either to wait for the occasional exhibition or to visit one of the many dealers specializing in the subject. The number of sporting paintings on public exhibition were very few; the Tate Gallery had a handful, the Walker Gallery in Liverpool had rather more, but these were kept unseen in the vaults. Leicester Art Gallery had some by Ferneley, but that was about all. Due mainly to the activities of the British Sporting Art Trust, the situation has changed considerably for the better in the last decade.

The National Art Collections Fund was formed in 1903 to help stem the export of our treasures abroad. At that time the Treasury Department's attitude was that there would be no demand for sporting pictures from abroad. It was not until 1924 that a plea for a national collection was made by that popular historian of sporting art, Walter Shaw Sparrow. He drew attention in his book, *British Sporting Artists*, to the need for a National Collection of Empire Sports. By 1926 it had become obvious to observers in the picture trade, such as A. C. R. Carter, editor for 55 years of *The Year's Art*, that the Treasury was wrong and that there was a growing cult for hunting and racing pictures in California and Kentucky. He deplored the omission of sporting pictures in the National Gallery.

The recommendations of the Royal Commission on National Museums and Galleries (1935) 'that no further time be lost in making acquisitions to fill the deplorable gaps at Trafalgar Square (National Gallery)', resulted in only a minor flurry of activity when a small gallery of sporting paintings of the English school, lent by H. Arthurton and Mrs Carstairs, was opened for a year at the Tate Gallery.

In the aftermath of the Second World War new hope was born when, in 1949, Walter Hutchinson opened the National Gallery of British Sports and Pastimes at Derby House, Stratford Place. There were 618 paintings and although some were of doubtful authenticity or wrongly attributed, nonetheless there was a nucleus of first class works that could have been developed into a National Collection. Alas, in forming it, Mr Hutchinson overspent and disaster followed. The gallery closed and the paintings were sold by Christie's in 1951–2. The bad publicity attached to this failure was compounded by the behaviour of our leading sporting artist and President of the Royal Academy, Sir Alfred Munnings. He revived the annual Royal Academy dinner, a grand occasion with Winston Churchill, Academician Extraordinary, and the Archbishop of Canterbury as guests. For the first time the speeches were broadcast live on radio, and it was an ideal occasion for the quiet promotion of sporting art. Inappropriately Sir

A Kill in Ashdown Park by James Seymour, 1743. Purchased by the Tate Gallery.

Alfred used it for an intemperate attack on the moderns. However well received it may have been by the majority of the public, it infuriated the critics and the leaders of the art establishment.

A prejudice against sporting art has been latent since the days of Sir Joshua Reynolds. This insult to the fashionable movements of the day made such dislike respectable and has not yet been forgotten or forgiven (the scabrous reviews of the 1987 Munnings exhibition in *The Times* and *The Guardian* are recent examples of this blinkered perception). The time could not have been more inappropriate for a pressure group intent on forming a national collection.

It was a particularly bad time for interest to falter, as two Americans were intent on buying sporting paintings. Paul Mellon, a sophisticated and cultured Anglophile, was building one of the world's great collections of English art. Against him in the auction rooms was cattle breeder Jack Dick, determined to have the finest assemblage of sporting paintings. Prices escalated to unimagined heights.

148

In the 1950s and 1960s the professed admirers of sporting art scarcely raised a voice of protest at the sacking of our heritage. In 1972, Stella Walker's masterly *Sporting Art, England, 1700–1900* reminded all those interested of what the country was steadily losing (although her publishers thought it prudent to omit references to a national collection). There followed, in 1974, the greatest exhibition of sporting art yet seen, arranged by the Arts Council at the Hayward Gallery. Few who saw it can have left without the belief that there was an aspect of art worth saving and it was probably no coincidence that in the same year the Tate Gallery's annual report appealed for more sporting art for the Historic British Collection.

In 1975 the idea of a Trust was born. The steering committee searched unsuccessfully for both gallery and finance but it soon became evident that there would be no quick and easy solution. Remembering the Tate Gallery's annual report, the director, Sir Norman Reid, and the Keeper of the Historic Collection, Dr Martin Butlin, were approached, and an association with the Trust resulted. The latter would seek sporting paintings, the Tate Gallery would accept the best for the National Collection and hang them in a sporting gallery. It was very much an act of faith. There was no money and there were no pictures.

The British Sporting Art Trust's Vestey Gallery at the National Horseracing Museum, Newmarket.

The British Sporting Art Trust was officially launched in 1977 and has been a success story. The first to give paintings to the Trust was Lady Price who presented *A Pointer* and *A Spaniel* by George Stubbs. This was followed by a typically generous gift by Paul Mellon, through the Trust, of 30 paintings, to the Tate Gallery. Two years later, 16 paintings were bequeathed to the Trust by Mrs Ambrose Clark of New York. The third major acquisition was the purchase by the Trust of 100 sporting engravings from the British Council. Acquisitions have continued and in one year these consisted of two paintings by Schwanfelder, one by George Morland, three by Lionel Edwards, one by Gilbert Holiday, a bronze by Cecil Brown, an engraving after J. F. Herring Snr and two photolithographs also after Holiday. Since 1986 the Trust have had the use of a gallery at the National Horseracing Museum at Newmarket, sponsored by Edmund Vestey, and that, together with the Tate's own sporting gallery, has resulted in the continued display of these paintings.

The Trust also serves those interested in sporting art in other ways. It has published two books, *A Bibliography of Sporting Artists* by Noral Titley and an *Inventory of Sporting Art Painting in Public Galleries in the United Kingdom* by Gerald Pendred. It has issued 15 essays on sporting artists and forwarded to members a bi-annual newsletter giving details of exhibitions, acquisitions and information. It has made grants to galleries seeking to purchase sporting paintings, presented a yearly prize for the best sculpture at the Society of Equestrian Artists Exhibition, organised an annual lecture, arranged visits to collections in England and abroad and started a library at York City Art Gallery. In 1987 a grant was awarded for post-graduate study of sporting art. In the United States

Steeplechase Cracks by J. F. Herring Snr, the property of HM Queen Elizabeth the Queen Mother. Loaned to the British Sporting Art Trust for an exhibition at the Fermoy Art Gallery, King's Lynn, Norfolk.

150

a sister organisation *The Friends of British Sporting Art* has been formed and with them it is hoped soon to develop a full programme of exchange.

As to the future, it seems inevitable that the price of good sporting paintings will continue to rise and the money available to foreign museums will mean that many will go abroad. The export of a number of these may be halted, provided that they meet the criteria of the reviewing committee, namely value in excess of £16,000, their presence in England for the last 50 years and being a works of 'national importance'. This does not, of course, guarantee that, at the end of the day, the money will be available to equal the offer by the foreign buyer.

While the tax laws do provide incentives for private treaty sales to museums, they do not match the generous terms in the USA, where, provided a painting is bequeathed to a public gallery its value is totally tax deductable. The finance available through the NACF and the Heritage Memorial Fund is finite and liable to change. The job of acquiring good representative examples of all periods of sporting paintings, engravings and sculptures will continue to be the most difficult and important function of the Trust. Our programmes to promote interest and research into the subject will, we hope, bring us more gifts, bequests, members and sponsors to enable us to continue the work. It will also, we believe, help to create an ambience in which contemporary sporting art will thrive.

Interior of a stable with running horses by James Seymour, *c*1745.

SOME GALLERIES SPECIALISING IN SPORTING ART

Arthur Ackermann & Son Ltd
33 New Bond Street, London W1Y 9HD
Tel: 01-493 3288
> *Seventeenth to twentieth century sporting
> paintings and watercolours. Sporting prints
> 1700–1880.*

Julian Armytage
The Old Rectory, Wayford, Nr Crewkerne,
Somerset TA18 8QG   Tel: 0460-73449
> *Eighteenth and nineteenth century sporting prints.
> Particular interest in racing subjects.*

Burlington Gallery Ltd
10 Burlington Gardens, London W1X 1LG
Tel: 01-734 9228
> *Engravings of eighteenth, nineteenth and
> twentieth centuries of all sports. All works of Cecil
> Aldin.*

Clifford Gallery
11 Market Place, Woburn MK17 9PZ
Tel: 0525-290355
> *Sporting and wildlife paintings, prints and
> bronzes, featuring living artists and sculptors.*

The Countryman's Gallery
Kibworth Harcourt, Leicestershire LE8 0NE
Tel: 053753-3211
> *Sporting and country pictures, prints and books,
> from 1890s – Edwards, Aldin, 'Snaffles' always
> available.*

The Court Gallery
8 Lancashire Court, 122–123 New Bond Street,
London W1   Tel: 01-409 1806
> *Twentieth century sporting pictures and prints
> especially works by and after 'Snaffles'.*

Cox and Company
37 Duke Street, London SW1
Tel: 01-930 1387
> *Nineteenth and twentieth century sporting
> paintings.*

Frost & Reed Ltd
41 New Bond Street, London W1Y 0JJ
Tel: 01-629 2457
> *Nineteenth and twentieth century sporting
> paintings: especially Munnings and the Herrings.*

Richard Green Gallery
44 Dover Street, London W1X 4JQ and
44 New Bond Street, London W1Y 9PE
Tel: 01-493 3939
> *Seventeenth to twentieth century sporting
> paintings.*

John and Judith Head, A.B.A.
The Barn Book Supply, 88 Crane Street, Salisbury,
Wilts   Tel: 0722-27767
> *Antiquarian books on angling, shooting, horse,
> deer-stalking, falconry. Signed prints and originals
> of 'Snaffles', Edwards, Munnings and Klaus Philipp.*

Heale Gallery
Heale Wold, Curry Rivel, Somerset TA10 0PQ
Tel: 0458-251 134
> *Sporting paintings and prints from 1800. Good
> selection of hunting and steeplechasing items.
> Original works by Michael Lyne always stocked.*

Malcolm Innes Gallery
172 Walton Street, London, SW3 2JL and
67 George Street, Edinburgh EM2 2JG
Tel: (London) 01-584 0575/5559,
(Edinburgh) 031-226 4151
> *Nineteenth and twentieth century Scottish
> sporting and landscape pictures and prints.*

Oscar & Peter Johnson Ltd
Lowndes Lodge Gallery, 27 Lowndes Street, London SW1
Tel: 01-235 6464
> *Eighteenth and nineteenth century sporting
> paintings.*

The Keyser Gallery at Farlow's
4 Royal Opera Arcade, Pall Mall, London SW1Y 4UY
Tel: 01-925 0203
> *Sporting pictures with emphasis on fishing and
> stalking subjects.*

Lacy Gallery
38–40 Ledbury Road, London W11 2AB
Tel: 01-229 9105/5316
Eighteenth and nineteenth century sporting, horse and other animal paintings/sculpture and sporting prints.

Lane Fine Art Ltd
86–88 Pimlico Road, London SW1W 8PL
Tel: 01-730 7374
English sporting oil paintings 1700–1840.

Thomas Lethbridge
185–186 Piccadilly, (Swaine/Adeney), London SW1
Tel: 01-734 4277
Sporting paintings, prints eighteenth to twentieth century.

McConnel Mason Gallery
14 Duke Street, London SW1Y 6DB
Tel: 01-839 7693
English eighteenth and nineteenth century sporting paintings.

McTague of Harrogate
17–19 Cheltenham Mount, Harrogate,
North Yorkshire HG1 1DW   Tel: 0423-67086
Eighteenth and nineteenth century sporting and animal prints, some paintings.

Marlborough Sporting Gallery
6 Kingsbury Street, Marlborough, Wilts
Tel: 0672-54074
Oils, watercolours and illustrated books. 1780– present day, especially Aldin, Edwards, 'Snaffles'.

Sally Mitchell
Thornlea Askham, Newark, Notts. NG22 0RN
Tel: 0778-3234
Limited edition sporting prints and paintings by contemporary sporting artists.

Newmarket Fine Art Inc
Suite 1, Allied House, Crown Walk, Newmarket,
Suffolk CB8 8LB   Tel: 0638-660065
Racing prints, pictures, caricatures, bronzes, specialising in the work of Klaus Philipp and bronzes by Barry Foley; specialist in mail order.

Newmarket Gallery
156 High Street, Newmarket
Suffolk   Tel: 0638-661183
Racing and field sport paintings, drawings, prints and memorabilia.

The Osborne Studio Gallery
The Carriage Hall, 29 Floral Street, London WC2
Tel: 01-836 5040
Contemporary sporting paintings, watercolours and prints and James Osborne's sporting bronzes, specialises in racing subjects.

Pawsey & Payne
90 Jermyn Street, London SW1Y 6JD   Tel: 01-930 4221
Eighteenth and nineteenth century English sporting paintings.

Richmond Gallery
8 Cork Street, London W1X 1PB   Tel: 01-437 9422
Contemporary oil paintings of racing and polo.

Rutland Gallery
32a George Street, London W1R 9FA
Tel: 01-459 5636
English primitive sporting and animal paintings.

The Sladmore Gallery
32 Bruton Place, Berkeley Square, London W1X 7AA
Tel: 01-499 0365
Nineteenth and twentieth century bronze animal sculpture.

Tryon Gallery Ltd
23–24 Cork Street, London W1X 1HB
Tel: 01-734 6961/2256
Natural history and sporting paintings, prints, bronzes and books of the nineteenth and twentieth centuries.

R. E. & G. B. Way, A.B.A.
Brettons, Burrough Green, Newmarket,
Suffolk CB8 9WA   Tel: 063-876 217
Antiquarian and secondhand books on hunting, horses and field sports.

Wingfield Sporting Gallery
55 Old Town Clapham, London SW4 0JQ
Tel: 01-622 6301
Sporting art, both traditional and contemporary.

SELECT BIBLIOGRAPHY

Aldin, Cecil, *Time I was Dead*, Eyre and Spottiswoode, 1934.

Apperley, C. J., ('Nimrod'), *Nimrod's Hunting Reminiscences*, John Lane, The Bodley Head, 1926 (reprint).

Apsley, Lady, *Bridleways Through History*, Hutchinson, 1936.

Armour, G. D., *Bridle and Brush, Reminiscences of a Sporting Artist*, Ashford, 1986 (reprint).

Baillie-Grohman, W. A., *Sport in Art from the 15th to the 18th Century*, Ballantyne, 1914.

Barrow, C., *Monarchy and the Chase*, Eyre and Spottiswoode, 1948.

Beckett, Oliver, *J. F. Herring and Sons*, J. A. Allen, 1981.

Bovill, E. W., *The England of Nimrod and Surtees, 1815–1854*, Oxford University Press, 1959.

Bromley Davenport, W., *Sport*, Maclehose, 1933.

Coombs, David, *Sport and the Countryside*, Phaidon, 1978.

Bury, A., *Joseph Crawhall, The Man and the Artist*, Skilton, 1958.

Edwards, Lionel, *Scarlet and Corduroy*, Putnam, 1941.
    Reminiscences of a Sporting Artist, Putnam 1947.

Egerton, Judy, *The Paul Mellon Collection, British Sporting and Animal Paintings, 1655–1867*, Tate Gallery, 1978.

Ellis, C. D. B., *Leicestershire and the Quorn Hunt*, Backus, 1951.

Falk, B., *Thomas Rowlandson, His Life and Work*, Hutchinson, 1949.

Fountain, Robert and Gates, Alfred, *Stubbs's Dogs*, Ackermann, 1984.

Gilbey, Sir Walter, *Animal Painters of England from the Year 1650*, 3 Vols., Vinton, 1900.
    The Life of George Stubbs R.A., Vinton, 1898.

Gilbey, Sir W. and Cuming E. D., *George Morland, His Life and Works*, Black, 1907.

Goldman, Paul, *Sporting Life: An Anthology of British Sporting Prints*, British Museum, 1983.

Grundy, C. R., *James Ward* R.A., Otto, 1909.

Hardy, R. F. H., *English Sport*, Country Life, 1932.

Hayes, John, *Rowlandson*, Phaidon, 1972.

Heron, Roy, *Cecil Aldin, The Story of a Sporting Artist*, Webb and Bower, 1981.

Horswell, Jane, *The Bronze Sculptures of the Animaliers*, Art Collector's Club, 1971.

Keith, E. C. and Thorburn, Archibald, *A Countryman's Creed*, Country Life, 1938.

Kendall, George E., *Notes on the Life of John Wootton, with a List of Engravings after his Pictures*, The Walpole Society Vol. XXII, Oxford, 1933.

Lane, Charles, *Sporting Aquatints and Engravings*, 2 vols., F. Lewis, 1978.
    Cooper Henderson and the Open Road, 1803–77, J. A. Allen, 1984.

Laver, James, *English Sporting Prints*, Ward Lock, 1970.

Mackay Smith, Alexander, *The Racehorses of America, 1832–72: Portraits and Other Paintings, by Edward Troye*, National Museum of Racing, New York, 1981.

MacClausland, H., *The English Carriage*, Batsford, 1948.

Messum, D., *Life and Work of Lucy Kemp-Welch*, Antique Collectors Club, 1976.

Meyer, Arlnie, *John Wootton*, Iveagh Bequest, Kenwood, 1984.

Mitchell, Sally, *A Dictionary of British Equestrian Artists*, Antique Collectors Club, 1985.

Mortimer, R., *The Jockey Club*, Cassell, 1958.

Munnings, Sir Alfred, Autobiography, 3 Vols; *An Artist's Life, The Second Burst* and *The Finish*, Museum Press.

Muir, J. B., *The Engraved Works of J. F. Herring Snr*, Fine Art Sporting Gallery, 1893.

Noakes, Aubrey, *Sportsmen in a Landscape*, Bodley Head, 1954.
    Ben Marshall, 1768–1835, F. Lewis, 1978.
    The World of Henry Alken, Witherby, 1952.

Ormond, Richard, *Sir Edwin Landseer*, Philadelphia Museum of Art, 1982, Tate Gallery, 1982.

Paget, Major Guy, *The Melton Mowbray of John Ferneley*, Backus, 1931. Scribner, New York, 1931.

Parker, C-A., *Mr Stubbs the Horse Painter*, J. A. Allen, 1971.

Pavière, S. H., *A Dictionary of Sporting British Painters*, F. Lewis, 1965.

Pendred, Gerald, *Inventory of Sporting Art Paintings in the Public Galleries in the United Kingdom*, British Sporting Art Trust and Boydell & Brewer, 1987.

Romford, T., *Famous Sporting Prints*, The Studio, 1927.

Sabin, V. P., *An Illustrated Catalogue of a Fine Collection of Old Sporting Prints*, Frank T. Sabin, 1933.

Selway, N. C., *The Regency Road*, Faber, 1957.

> *The Golden Age of Coaching as Depicted by James Pollard*, F. Lewis, 1972.

Shaw Sparrow, W., *British Sporting Artists*, Bodley Head, 1922.

  Angling in British Art, Bodley Head, 1923.

  Henry Alken, Williams and Norgate, 1927. Scribner, New York, 1927.

  British Sporting Painters, Bodley Head, 1931.

  George Stubbs and Ben Marshall, Cassell, 1939.

Siltzer, Captain Frank, *The Story of British Sporting Prints*, Halton and Truscott Smith, 1929.

Snaffles, *A Half Century of Memories*, Collins, 1949.

Taylor, Basil, *Animal Paintings in England from Barlow to Landseer*, Penguin, 1958.

Taylor, Basil, *Stubbs*, Phaidon, 1971. Harper and Row, New York, 1971.

Tidy, G., *A Little about Leech*, Constable, 1931.

Titley, Norah M., *A Bibliography of British Sporting Artists*, British Sporting Art Trust and Sotheby's, 1985.

Walker, Stella, *Sporting Art, England 1700–1900*, Studio Vista, 1972.

Watson, J. N. P., *Lionel Edwards, Master of the Sporting Scene*, Sportsman's Press, 1986.

Wilder, F. L., *English Sporting Prints*, Thames and Hudson, 1974.

Wood, J. C., *A Dictionary of British Animal Painters*, Lewis, 1973.

INDEX